Permutation Design

In design, the problems that designers are called upon to solve can be regarded as problems of permutations. A permutation is an ordered arrangement of elements in a set. In our case, the set is design and the elements are design components, such as lines, shapes, forms, or spaces.

Traditionally, such arrangements are done by human designers who base their decision-making process either on intuition or on random sampling until a valid solution is found. However, in both cases the solution found may be an acceptable one but cannot be labeled as "the best possible solution" due to the subjective or arbitrary nature of the selection process. In contrast, by harnessing the potential of computational design, these elements can be arranged in all possible ways and then the best ones can be chosen based on specific criteria. By presenting a complete list of permutation-based arrangements the "best solution" will eventually reveal itself by excluding all other possible solutions.

This book comprehensively addresses theories, techniques, and examples of permutation design in order to fully demonstrate to the reader the full range of possibilities this method represents. The significance of such an approach to design is enormous, paradigmatic, and far-reaching. It provides an alternative method for design analysis, synthesis, and evaluation that is based on computational force rather than pure human intelligence alone. In contrast to human-based random sampling or intuition, permutation-based design offers the assurance of an optimum design since any possible alternative design can be eliminated. From a practical point of view, this methodology offers a paradigmatic shift away from the current state of design practice where arbitrariness, repetition, and redundancy often exist. From a theoretical viewpoint, this new paradigm may offer alternative insights into the value of human creativity, intuition, and intelligence.

Kostas Terzidis was an Associate Professor at Harvard University Graduate School of Design from 2003 until 2012. He taught courses in Algorithmic Architecture, Kinetic Architecture, Digital Media, and Design Research Methods. He holds a PhD in Architecture from the University of Michigan (1994), a M.Arch from OS (1989), and a Diploma of Engineering from the Aristotle University in Thessaloniki, Greece (1986). He is now the CEO and co-founder of Organic Parking, a company developing smart city parking space optimization using mobile social networks.

Permutation Design

Buildings, Texts, and Contexts

Kostas Terzidis

LONDON AND NEW YORK

First published 2015
by Routledge
2 Park Square, Milton Park, Abingdon, Oxon OX14 4RN

and by Routledge
711 Third Avenue, New York, NY 10017

Routledge is an imprint of the Taylor & Francis Group, an informa business

© 2015 Kostas Terzidis

The right of Kostas Terzidis to be identified as author of this work has been asserted by him in accordance with sections 77 and 78 of the Copyright, Designs and Patents Act 1988.

All rights reserved. No part of this book may be reprinted or reproduced or utilized in any form or by any electronic, mechanical, or other means, now known or hereafter invented, including photocopying and recording, or in any information storage or retrieval system, without permission in writing from the publishers.

Trademark notice: Product or corporate names may be trademarks or registered trademarks, and are used only for identification and explanation without intent to infringe.

British Library Cataloguing-in-Publication Data
A catalogue record for this book is available from the British Library

Library of Congress Cataloging-in-Publication Data
Terzidis, Kostas, 1962-
　Permutation design : buildings, texts and contexts / Kostas Terzidis.
　　pages cm
　Includes bibliographical references and index.
　1. Architectural design—Data processing. 2. Decision making—Data processing. 3. Computer-aided design. I. Title.
　NA2728.T475 2014
　720—dc23
　　　　　　　　　　　　　　　　　　2014001460

ISBN: 978-0-415-64449-5 (hbk)
ISBN: 978-0-415-64450-1 (pbk)
ISBN: 978-1-315-79591-1 (ebk)

Typeset in Minion
by Keystroke, Station Road, Codsall, Wolverhampton

Printed and bound in Great Britain by
TJ International Ltd, Padstow, Cornwall

To my mother, Ismini,
for challenging my certainties

– CONTENTS –

Introduction, 1

<u>ONE</u>
The Myth of the Genius, 17

<u>TWO</u>
Parasight(s), 37

<u>THREE</u>
Digital Culture: A Critical View, 59

<u>FOUR</u>
Combinations, Permutations, and Other Predicaments, 97

1. Geometrical Permutations, 101
2. Network Topology Permutations, 107

<u>FIVE</u>
Studies, 113

Epi(dia)logue, 145
Index, 159

 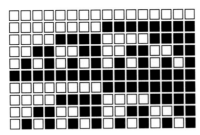 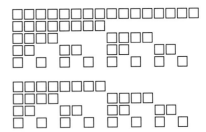

Introduction

Designers and artists express their ideas by developing imaginary worlds before they project them as images on a drafting board or a canvas. In their minds, they create an ideal world, a world that fits their needs and expresses their desires. By creating systems of symbols and rules, designers are able to describe, represent, and control their imaginary worlds. In architecture, for instance, the construction and development of significant buildings was usually preceded or paralleled by theoretical projects which were never built, either because they were too impractical or because their purpose was to be used as ideal models and paradigms to be followed. By formulating such models, theorists were able to express their theoretical views about architecture, space, and society, to criticize the current practice, and to demonstrate how they imagine an ideal world. Perault, the architect of the peristyle of the Louvre, argued that architecture is a fantastic art of pure invention.[1] He asserted that architecture really exists in the mind of the designer and that there is no connection to the natural world. In addition, architecture as an imaginative art obeys its own rules which are internal and personal to each designer, and that is why most creators are vaguely aware of the rules of nature and yet produce excellent pieces of art.

The purpose of an ideal model in architecture is not necessarily the actual production of a building. Many models serve merely the purpose of fulfilling the designer's imagination and satisfying his/her need to create a perfect world. On the other hand, models, such as mathematical, social, and statistical, are rational constructions, which are supposed to describe real-life phenomena. By altering the parameters that describe those models one is able to interpolate and extrapolate the data and understand their behavior. Moreover, alterations under extreme conditions reveal behavior far more unpredictable than a human mind can imagine.

In mathematics, notions such as randomness, reality, and imagination have been extensively investigated. The fact that in nature certain phenomena have a possibility of existence that cannot be predicted gives rise to the concept of *randomness*. A one-to-one correspondence of natural objects to discrete representations in our minds defines the world of *reality*. Finally, the absence of a fact or an evidence of reality gives rise to the concept of *imagination*. In imagination, we do not know the nature of the elements we are dealing with; we are only sure about the relationships that determine their behavior. Elements such as infinity, zero, and the square root of minus one are objects of imagination. Unlike random elements, the existence of imaginary elements cannot be explained, but their behavior can be described through rational relationships.

Parallel with the history of architecture is the history of media technology by which abstract entities such as events, experiences, and ideas become symbolically represented and transmitted through electronic devices. Through the use of mathematical models, it has become possible to visualize those abstract entities, verify their existence, and project their behavior into a once unimaginable world. The introduction of new electronic media in the last sixty years gave a different twist to the exploration of these mathematical notions. The ideas of mathematical models and simulations were realized through fast computations and large memory capacities. A world was *discovered*, the world of *simulations*, which is a "make-believe" representation of mathematical models. This world can be projected to the computer screen or animated through real-time computations. Objects, represented through instructions in the computer's memory, were projected to a screen by simple algorithms, then transformed as if they were physically there, occasionally dressed in fancy textures and, in special cases, animated and transformed indefinitely.

Since the invention of the digital computer, theorists strive to find ways to relate computers to human thinking. Computers are arithmetic devices, which can perform all basic arithmetic operations, such as addition, subtraction, multiplication, and so on. By combining basic operations computers are also able to perform complex algebraic operations and derive accurate results in minimum time. Furthermore and most importantly, computers have the ability to operate as logical devices, in the sense that they can perform logical operations, such as IF, THEN, ELSE, AND, OR, and so on. Given a number of truth tables, computers are able to verify the truth or falsity of a logical sentence or expression and therefore to determine the validity of an argument. This latter capability led computer theorists to inquire whether those arguments could be compatible to problems taken from the real world. In other words, whether it is possible to develop cognitive mechanisms, which would process information from the real world and derive answers or propose solutions, as if they were carried out by human beings. Some theorists expect to see even more than that. They expect to see computers, which would be able to simulate human thinking to a degree such that they would perform tasks, which are considered by humans to be highly intellectual, such as design.

Design is a mental process that has puzzled people for many years. It is a process that everybody knows when one sees it happen but is hard to know how it is done exactly. The design process has divided people into two extreme positions on how it is performed. Many tend to feel that when one designs a product, or a house, or a poster, that the designer "follows his heart" and it is impossible to find out what is going on in the human mind during the design process. They also tend to go as far as to say that if a designer tries to reveal or describe the process of creation this will spoil the purity of the process and the designer will not be able to design that way again.

On the other extreme, there are people who think that design is a rational process regardless of whether the particular designer can express it in words or not. They believe that when a designer creates something, the designer follows a series of steps, rules, or tactics that are very logical. In that sense, diagrams, flowcharts, and algorithms can be created to depict and re-create the design process. Computers tend to be a great tool for these believers, because as rational machines they can be programmed to perform the same steps as those of the designers. The only thing that needs to be done is to find, codify, and feed the computer with those steps, rules, and tactics and then design will occur. This however has not happened yet. No computer can design as well as a human designer, or so the experts say.

At the same time, many designers admit that they reach limits during the design process. What they have in mind often cannot be drawn with their own traditional tools. As a consequence, the truth may lie in-between. Computers can be programmed to do things that designers can then use to enhance the design process. For example, computational design is one way of using computers during the design process as a medium to design better or different. It uses the computational and combinatorial power of a computer to generate schemes that can be useful to designers. It can also help designers synthesize forms, alter their shapes, and combine solids in ways often unpredictable. Computer graphics, on the other hand, is used as a way of depicting the end product so realistically that even the best artist cannot paint that fast and/or accurately. Computer graphics uses the computer screen as a means of projecting a complex world that either resembles the real world we live in or is completely based on imagination. One of the original main objectives of computer graphics was to simulate reality as close as possible. Light, color, motion, facial expression, anything that is associated with the real world can be codified and re-enacted in a computer-simulated world. At the same time, alteration of the real world led to imaginary conditions that are also important in computer graphics. Fractals, morphing, or grammars are methods that cannot be found per se in the real world, and as such are imaginary.

To identify the problem of design in general it is necessary first to define the term *design*. While many definitions and models of design exist, most agree that design is a process of inventing physical things which display new physical order, organization, form, in response to function. However, since no formula or predetermined steps exist which can translate form and function into a new, internally consistent physical entity, design has been held to be an art rather than a science. It is considered to be an iterative, "trial-and-error" process that relies heavily on knowledge, experience, and intuition. Intuition became a basis of many design theories, often referred to as "black box" theories. According to them, design, as well as its evaluation, tends to be highly subjective.

In contrast, another set of theories defines the design process as a rational *problem-solving process*. According to the latter, design can be conceived as a systematic, organized, rational activity. As defined by researchers over the past fifty years, for every problem there exists a solution space; that is, a domain that includes all the possible solutions to a problem. If design is seen as a problem-solving activity, the theory implies that there is a design solution that can be invented. Problem solving can be characterized as a process of searching through alternative solutions in this space to discover one or several which meet certain goals and may, therefore, be considered *solution states*. The way by which the design problem will be solved can be either deterministic or probabilistic but always possible.

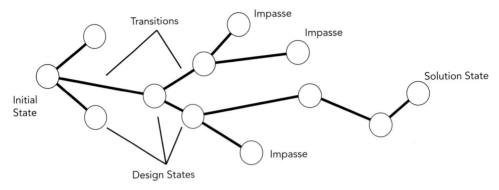

0.1 Design stages during the design process

In the early 1960s, Alexander published a highly influential book titled *Notes on the Synthesis of Form*.[2] In it Alexander quotes the need for rationality in the design process. If design, he argues, is a conceptual interaction between form and context, there may be a way to improve it by making an abstract picture of the problem, which will retain only its abstract structural features. As a mathematician, he introduced set theory, structural analysis, and the theory of algorithms as tools for addressing the design problem. He asserted that even quality issues could be represented by binary variables. If a misfit occurs, the variable takes the value 1; if not, 0. Each binary variable stands for one possible kind of misfit between form and context. This approach was followed by a flurry of related research into the problem. However, Alexander's contribution was much more far-reaching. He introduced computers into the design process by suggesting which aspects of the design process are amenable to systematization and which are not. Further, he suggested that the design process entails frequent changes of mind (or changes of constraints, in scientific terms) and that a system should permit these changes to occur.

Traditionally, design is a mental process of arranging parts in a way that is most efficient, attractive, and/or meaningful. Even though design seems to be a mental function with an end product it differs significantly from discipline to discipline. In product design, emphasis is placed not only on the efficiency of the end product but also on the aesthetic value of it. In architectural design, function is an important factor in the design process but the form of the building is also very important. In engineering, often the design process can become very rational and design decisions can be made entirely on cost and efficiency.

The design of a product, for example, involves a concept formation, decision strategies, operations analysis, and research methods. *The concept formation* phase of any design project is probably one of the most difficult to define and manage. It includes brainstorming, morphological analysis, and prototyping. The *decision strategies* are used to assess and evaluate situations as a basis for making decisions. Some of the methods are designed for use by experts or a small group of experts. This phase includes decision analysis and value analysis. The *operations analysis* is used to model or study the behavior of a design, or a particular aspect of a design. It can be applied to an existing system, to study its behavior, or to one that is being developed, to model how it will behave in the future. It includes flow models, heuristic models, input-output models, interaction analysis, network analysis, optimization models, sequence analysis, simulation, and task analysis. The *research methods* are used to gather, investigate, assess, and verify information related to the needs of a design. They can be used to research the content needs of the design as well as the needs defining the context of that design. They include experimental models, focus groups, knowledge search, technology assessment, usability testing, and user surveys.

The introduction of computers capable of carrying out complex tasks led eventually to their inclusion in the "design process" debate. One of artificial intelligence's focuses is in the development of algorithms and methods that will codify the process of design. If and when that happens computers can design on their own by simply following these algorithms and methods. Even though a complete computer design system has not been yet developed that could compete with a traditional human designer, the theory of how to codify design methods led to a new way of looking at design methods. These ways range from complete optimism, where a computer can design on its own, to realistic approaches, where the computer functions as tools for the human designer. In the following sections we will describe briefly some of these attempts.

With the introduction of the first relatively complex computers, theorists investigated the possibility of self-designing machines. They thought that one of the areas where the computer could be helpful to a designer could be in automatic design; that is, in finding a large number of possible schemes at a sufficiently early stage of the design process, and choosing the best one for further development. An early attempt was systems, which could be used to describe spaces that might go into a building, indicating their dimensions, their arrangement, and their materials. The computer then arranged the spaces solving the problem. This approach has been used extensively ever after for solving complex design problems that are related to arranging parameters in optimum locations. These approaches focus on the functionality of the end design product and do not take into account aesthetic or artistic parameters. In areas such as design of computer chips, nuclear plants, or hospitals automatic spatial allocation plays a very important role today.

Some theorists have argued that many problems cannot be solved algorithmically, either because the procedure leading to their solution is ill defined or because not all the information needed to solve them is available or accurate. Such problems make it necessary to use *heuristic and adaptive decision procedures*. Heuristic methods typically rely on trial-and-error techniques to arrive at a solution. Such techniques are, by definition, much closer to the *search-and-evaluate* processes used in architectural design. In adaptive procedures, the computer itself learns by experience, which could follow a procedure, and, at the same time, could discern and assimilate conversational idiosyncrasies. Such a mechanism, after observing a user's behavior, could reinforce the dialogue by using a predictive model to respond in a manner consistent with personal behavior and idiosyncrasies. The dialogue would be so intimate such as that of a close and wise friend assisting in the design process.

In systems, known as *expert systems*, knowledge about a specific area of human expertise is codified as a set of rules. By means of dialogue with the user, the system arrives at a solution to a particular design problem. New knowledge is provided by the user to the knowledge base without a programmer having to rewrite or reconfigure the system. The ability of the system to justify conclusions and to explain reasoning leads to further systematization of the design process, but also, sometimes, to unpredictable behavior by the computer.

Historically, as a result of growing computer capabilities during the 1960s, automated design engendered a great number of expectations. Unfortunately, most of these expectations were not met, perhaps because machine intelligence was overestimated. Some types of design, such as architectural design, are much more complicated processes because they entail factors that cannot be codified or predicted. The heuristic processes that guide the search rely not only on information pertinent to the particular problem, but also on information which is indirectly related to it. In addition, the states that describe the design process do not exist before they are generated. Therefore, a solution state can only be identified "after the fact"; that is, after it has been generated.

These problems, as well as the computer needs of design offices, led to changes in the approach to automated design. Rather than emulating designers, the approach after the 1970s was predicated on the belief that they should be supported. The machine was introduced as an aid to instruction, as a mediator for the goals and aspirations of the designers. The computer could communicate with designers by accepting information, manipulating it, and providing useful output. In addition to synthesizing form, computers were also able to accept and process non-geometric information about form. These needs eventually led to the development of Computer-Aided Design (CAD).

Computer-Aided Design was developed to assist the designer during the design process. The assistance was in the form of drafting, modeling, rendering, and presentation. The first CAD systems date as early as the 1960s, with systems that could allow the user to draw, draft, and visualize some basic 3D models. Most of these systems were used in the automotive and aerospace engineering mainly because at that time they were the only ones that could afford such systems. With the popularization of the microcomputer and a significant fall in the prices, architects and graphics designers started to use CAD systems. One of the interesting debates in the 1970s was whether CAD was useful or not for these designers. This debate kept going on in the 1980s and today we can see that a majority of architectural and graphics design offices use computers in almost all phases of the design process. In most engineering areas, CAD became a valuable tool for design, evaluation, estimation, and optimization. CAD systems and interactive graphics are used to design components and systems of mechanical, electrical, electromechanical, and electronic devices, including structures such as buildings, automobile bodies, airplane and ship hulls, very large-scale-integrated (VLSI) chips, optical systems, and telephone and computer networks. Further, large and efficient database management led to the integration of data and geometry in the form of Building Information Management (BIM). Many CAD systems consequently transformed from geometrical systems to data-rich BIM systems where information is not only stored but also updated through Internet communication protocols.

As design began to be increasingly thought of as a systematic and rational activity, many of its empirical and experimental rules were explored. By operating on symbolic structures stored in the computer's memory and manipulating them according to rules, computers could reason about, or even predict, the behavior of a simulated environment. The machines were made to carry out a "make-believe" happening, a *simulation*. The purpose of a simulation is to use or operate on a model (often a mathematical model encoded in a computer program) to learn about the behavior of the reality being modeled. Numerous simulation models were formulated and much progress was made toward simulating design states. These models simulated the states of a designed environment and the transitions from one state to another. Yet, no model was formulated which could encompass both the relationships between the components of a design and its environment.

Computer graphics is related to design and simulation by being a method for display and visualization of design products or processes. Research in computer graphics can be divided into two general directions: representation of the known and representation of the unknown. In the first category, reality is the competition. In other words, research in this area focuses in finding ways of perfectly representing objects, scenes, or behaviors that can be found in the real world. Image processing and object representation fall into this area. In the second direction, focus is placed on representing objects and behaviors that are not known in advance. Simulation and procedural graphics fall into this category.

Representation of the known is based on techniques for representing the real world. The real world that surrounds us can be seen either as a projection of the retina of the eye or as existing in three dimensions as material forms. In the first case, computer graphics uses the surface of the computer screen as a medium for projection. Color samples from the real world are associated with tiny dots on the computer screen called pixels. By manipulating color intensities, hue, and saturation projected scenes can be displayed. Furthermore, by altering the values of the pixels one can analyze, synthesize, transform, and juxtapose the picture. In the second case, three-dimensional objects in the real world are abstracted as geometric forms and are codified in the computer's memory. This process is called *modeling*. As a result of modeling, objects are represented as geometric shapes, and then as numbers. Furthermore, models are rendered with textures, shades, and shadows to resemble their original objects as accurately as possible. The export of such data into the real world using sculpting or layering devices allows the creation of 3D physical objects through a process referred to as *fabrication*. In all these cases, the objective of representation is known: to depict as accurately as possible the real world.

Representation of the unknown is based on alterations of techniques used in the representation of the known. By observing structures and processes that hold together the real world, one can alter or extrapolate them obtaining unknown or unpredictable results. Simulation is the process of using or operating a model (often a mathematical model encoded in a computer program) to learn about the behavior of the reality being modeled. But simulations can be performed to learn about the unpredictable behavior of a reality being modeled, such as molecular or weather phenomena. Similarly, simulations can be performed to visualize imaginary scenarios, such as art and movies. These simulations allow us to see beyond reality and to experiment with imaginary structures and processes.

Computationalism is a term coined here to denote the theory that, through the use of computation, knowledge can be acquired that is impossible or foreign to the human mind. There are two terms that need to be defined here first: impossible and foreign. Impossible refers to the inability to predict a result due to a large number of calculations. Foreign refers to the inability to comprehend the results of such calculations. For example, the solution or visualization of a recursive equation (e.g. a quadratic polynomial) may reveal behaviors unpredictable and often unexplainable, yet true. The assertion of truth is based on the rational structure of computational schemes and their consequent characteristic of being coherent, traceable, and consistent. Computationalism assumes that intelligence, as a rational process of problem solving, is not an exclusive privilege of the human mind but rather can be abstracted as a generalized process, codified in the form of rules, and then re-implemented into another medium, i.e. binary, chemical, biological, etc. In other words, human intelligence is a biological instantiation of a more general structure that manifests itself in what we define as intelligence. Further, the implementation into an alternative medium takes advantage of the properties of that medium rendering results much faster, accurate, or complex. Most importantly, a human is able to compare one's own process with that of another's non-human as to detect similarities or differences in performance, but also to engage in mutual or parallel synergy as to share, complement, and enhance either process.

The process of confronting design as a structured problem has been discussed by many theorists in the area of artificial intelligence (AI) and many models have been developed and implemented. The main concern of those theorists is the degree to which design can be rationalized. One position is that design is an ill-structured problem, but it can be solved by considering not one, but a spectrum of alternative solutions and choosing the most satisfying one. In order to produce these alternative solutions, design has to be first viewed as a problem-solving process.

If the design process is viewed as *a problem-solving process*, design may be conceived as a far more systematic and rigorous activity. In that sense, for every problem a *solution space* exists. That is, a domain exists that includes all the possible solutions to the problem. Problem solving can then be characterized as the process of identifying and evaluating alternative solutions in this space in order to discover one or several which will meet certain goals and may be considered to be appropriate and desirable. Four such cases will be offered as food for thought below: game playing, problem solving, perception, and language.

In game playing, one of the objectives is to make intelligent moves. For example, in chess, there are rules, strategies, and tactics. Every move has to fulfill local and global goals. In design, we can also acknowledge the involvement of rules, strategies, and tactics during the design process. The question, however, is what are the goals in design? What is the local and what is the global goal? One of game playing's properties is that although people who do them well are considered to be intelligent, it appears that computers can perform well by simply exploring a large number of solution paths in a short time and then selecting the best. It seems that this process required little knowledge and could therefore be easily programmed. In other words, the computer's involvement in the design process does not have to be that of imitation rather than that of extension.

Problem solving is another area in which AI may be useful in design. It involves a beginning, a goal, and a strategy. Every move has to be analyzed extensively. By considering a set of logical possibilities, a solution strategy may eventually be found. To investigate this kind of reasoning, methods must be developed that incorporate matching, indexing, heuristics, generate-and-test, hill-climbing, and breadth-first searches. All of these methods are general and aim at solving a problem. The question is what are the problems of design? Can they be defined? What are the goals in design?

Perception is an area of AI that includes vision and speech. Perception tries to find out how we recognize patterns; how we see and hear. Perceptual tasks are difficult because they involve analog (rather than digital) signals. Typically noisy and usually a large number of things (some of which are obstructing others) must be perceived at once. Nonetheless, their contribution to intelligence is extremely significant since perception is our main link with the external world. Perception can contribute not only in the design process but also as a vehicle for understanding, recognizing, and criticizing design solutions. But what are the criteria for evaluating design? Can they be specified?

The ability to use language to communicate is an important medium that separates people from animals. The understanding of spoken language is extremely difficult since it includes the problems of perception. Even if we restrict the problem to written language it is still very difficult. This problem is also referred to as natural language understanding. In order to understand a sentence, it is not only necessary to incorporate knowledge about the language's structure (vocabulary, grammar, spelling, and syntax) but also to know about the topic discussed so that implied statements are understood. One of the problems of design is how designers communicate ideas. This involves not only the actual exchange of straightforward information, but the expressions, metaphors, gestures, sketches, etc. involved in conversations between designers. How AI can help designers communicate locally or remotely is an interesting undertaking, especially through the use of computer networks. Another area of design where natural language understanding may be useful is in the notion that design is a language of shapes. By analyzing natural languages is it possible to help designers compare and understand their formal languages?

Computationalism has fallen under criticism not for its methods or accomplishments but rather for its definitions and explanations. Terms such as understanding, decision, response, or even more mundane ones, such as knowing, winning, helping, or saying, involve an elementary level of consciousness, which computational devices do not possess. While human beings are very good at solving complex problems or artistic creation, computers are powerful processing devices with enormous memory capacities. What is the power of the machine? What is the power of the human? It seems that humans are good in processing high-level abstract information. Judgment, interpretation, and creativity are unique characteristics of human thought. On the other hand, humans are very slow in complex number calculations or in memorizing large amounts of information. Computers and humans seem to be superior in different areas of thought. Humans are good in using many rules and a few tasks; computers are good in using fewer rules and performing many tasks. The question that may be posed then is whether computers and humans can co-exist and whether they can complement one another.

As computers become more and more capable of performing many tasks at speeds that surpass by far human performance, it is important to ask what kind of relationship will humans and computers have in the future. In other words, as computer performance increases and their capabilities mimic those of humans, how can AI research relate to humans? What operations make a computer useful to a human? What computer operations are impossible for humans to perform? Three scenarios seem possible. The computer may:

1. Complement the human thinker.
2. Extend the process of thinking.
3. Replace the human thinker.

According to the first scenario, computers provide useful information, advise, appraise, and assist the designer. The goal of Computer-aided Design (CAD) and computer vision systems is to expand in this direction. Computers function mainly as tools for the designer and can help either during the design process or in the early stages of design. Expert systems are also available (an area of AI) whose goal is to assist the designer. Their target is to provide the designer with useful information and function as a consultant during the design process. The computer can be very useful in helping the designer meet the large number of constraints to be simultaneously considered in any design problem. Moreover, the complexity of the design problem can be so great that a designer would be unable to arrive at an appropriate solution unless a computer is used to break down the problem into sub-problems and use a computational approach to solve them.

According to the second scenario, the computer functions as a tool that allows the designer to explore alternative possibilities and extrapolate into unknown intellectual territories. Abstract entities, such as events, experiences, and ideas, can be symbolically represented and transmitted through electronic devices. It is possible to visualize those abstract entities, verify their existence, and project their behavior into a once unimaginable world through the use of mathematical models. The introduction of new electronic media in the last fifty years gave a different twist to the exploration of these mathematical notions. The ideas of mathematical models and simulations were first realized through fast computations and large memory capacities. A new world was *discovered*, the world of *virtual reality*, which is a "make-believe" representation of mathematical models. This world can be projected to the computer screen or animated through real-time computations. Objects, represented through instructions in the computer's memory, were projected to a screen by simple algorithms, then transformed as if they were physically there.

According to the third scenario, the intellectual capabilities of a computer may be far superior to those of the human designer. This scenario suggests a computer program may replace the designer. Since the invention of the digital computer, theorists strive to find ways to relate computers to human thinking. Computers' ability to perform logical operations led to the possibility of them operating as integrated logical devices. Given a number of truth tables, computers are able to verify the truth or falsity of a logical sentence and therefore to determine the validity of an argument. This latter capability led computer theorists to inquire whether those arguments could be compatible to problems taken from the real world. In other words, is it possible to develop cognitive mechanisms, which would process information from the real world and derive answers or propose solutions as if they were carried out by humans? Some theorists expect to see even more than that. They expect to see computers, which would be able to simulate human thinking to a degree such that they would perform tasks, which are considered by humans to be highly intellectual, even impossible. I am one of them.

This book is about permutations in design. A permutation is an ordered arrangement of elements in a set. In this case, the set is design and the elements are design components (lines, shapes, forms, colors, spaces, etc.) These elements are arranged in all possible ways (often billions and trillions of patterns) and then the best ones are chosen based on some criteria (function, efficiency, performance, price, etc.) This book sets out to develop theories, techniques, and examples that illustrate this possibility.

However, the book also goes beyond the technicalities and inquires into extreme computation in design as it projects into future possibilities. The vast power of computers to find all possible solutions and determine the best possible solution to a design problem implies also many other repercussions: determinism in design, infinite vs. finite, human vs. software contribution, putting bounds to the boundless imagination, and many more.

The book is composed of six chapters. The first chapter is titled "The Myth of the Genius". The intention of this chapter is to describe, analyze, and inquire about the humanistic paradigm of the genius and its consequences in contemporary design. The purpose is to offer a new alternative paradigm that involves the designer as a mediator of computational process, a meta-designer. In this paradigm, a more fair and equal relationship emerges for the computer and the human where each party offers its best in a synergy that leads to more than the addition of the parts.

The second chapter is titled "Parasight(s)". In this chapter the attempt is to introduce a new concept, that of a "parasight". A parasight is an intellectual idea that emerges through, on, or in the body of a theoretical structure by interpretation, mutation, and transgression. It is a hidden underlying intellectual scheme that feeds on the existing mode of thought. It serves as a means of alternative, foreign, or alien expressions that function as a critique to the existing intellectual status quo offering a reactive force against the overarching ideology.

Chapter three deals with the emerging field of digital culture. In this chapter the emergent notion of digital design is discussed. A critical view of computation in design is presented with references to common practices in schools of design. Advantages and disadvantages are presented. Permutations are shown as an alternative method of design. Finally, the author shows a series of experiments in the field of linguistics that lead toward an automatic compositional device that may function as a paradigm for generative design.

Chapter four is a brief tutorial that introduces, explains, and articulates the use of permutations in architectural design. It starts with the basic concepts from mathematics (i.e. combinatorial analysis, multi-variable permutations, network and topological permutations), and then venues into more complex algorithms that have a high potential value in design:

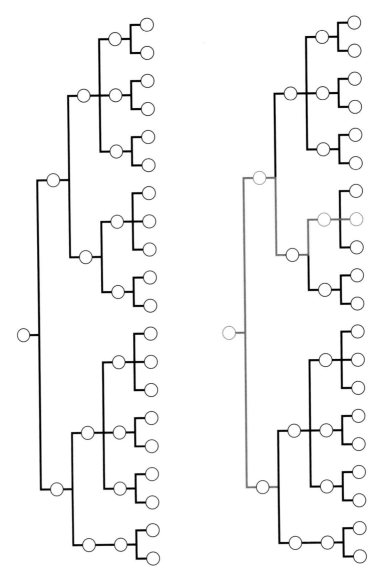

0.2 (a) All possible design stages in all possible design processes. (b) A particular series of design stages in a particular design process (shown in gray)

optimization, probability, and randomness. For each algorithm code, explanations and examples are given. The purpose of this chapter is to show, clarify, and demystify the creation of permutations and to provide some core examples that can be used as paradigms in different contexts.

The next chapter is an illustration of design work that uses algorithms introduced in the previous chapter. The themes addressed are hybrid, synergistic, and poetic because the purpose here is to show a combined logic between humans and computers as well as the limits of extreme computation and automation in design.

Finally, the last chapter is a stream of thoughts, reactions, and criticisms on the theses developed in this book. The discussion is presented in the format of dialogue between the author and students of architecture, design, and media arts. A series of ideas emerge in the course of the discussion ultimately establishing a collective critical framework and challenging not only the author's positions but also the current mainstream discourse. It provides constructive criticism to the book and sets possible new directions for the future.

The intent of this book is to use computation in its true capacity to address design problems. Most research in computational design is limited to computerization or imitations of human manual design. In contrast, this approach involves intense computation allowing designers to get into extreme, strange, and occasionally unpredictable situations. The scope is to produce exhaustive lists of possible combinations of elements in a building producing possible plans (sometimes billions and trillions) and then select the best ones from the list based on criteria such as budget, orientation, functionality, or aesthetics. The book covers technical issues related to permutations, philosophical topics arising from such extreme computations, and design permutations where the best results are shown (patterns, plans, 3D buildings).

In design, and, in particular, architectural design, the problem that designers are called upon to solve can be regarded as a problem of permutations, i.e. the rearrangement of design elements within a set of discrete positions (i.e. a grid) until a solution is found that satisfies a set of criteria. Traditionally, such arrangements are done by human designers who base their decision making either on intuition (from the point of view of the designer) or on random sampling until a valid solution is found. However, in both cases the solution found may be an acceptable one but cannot be labeled as "the best possible solution" due to the subjective or arbitrary nature of the selection process. In contrast, an exhaustive list of permutation-based arrangements will eventually reveal the "best solution" since it will exclude all other possible solutions.

The significance of such an approach to design is enormous, paradigmatic, and far-reaching. It provides an alternative method for design analysis, production, and evaluation that is based on computational force rather than pure human intelligence alone. In contrast to human-based random sampling or intuition, permutation-based design offers the assurance of an optimum design since any possible alternative design has been eliminated. From a practical point of view, the system offers a paradigmatic shift away from the current state of architectural practice where arbitrariness, repetition, and redundancy often exist. From a theoretical viewpoint, this new paradigm will offer alternative insights into the value of human creativity, intuition, and intelligence. At the same time, it will point out the enormous potential that computation plays in the field of design.

Additionally, architectural design is only one of the many possible uses of permutation-based design. Other fields of design can benefit from the permutation-based approach such as urban, landscape, mechanical, or industrial design, to name a few. However, architectural design has been chosen as a case study because of its complex nature, its portrayal as an exclusively human activity, and the long experience of this author with the subject. Theoretically, any discrete pattern can be analyzed or synthesized as a product of permutations. Given a design program and provided with enough computational power, increasingly more elaborate designs can be produced that will depend on and will test the current limits of computer power.

Notes

1. Boullée, E.-L., "Architecture, Essay on Art", in *Treatise on Architecture*, Rosenau, H. (ed.), Paris: MS Français Bibliotheque National, 1953, p. 83.
2. Alexander, C., *Notes on the Synthesis of Form*, Cambridge, MA: Harvard University Press, 1964.

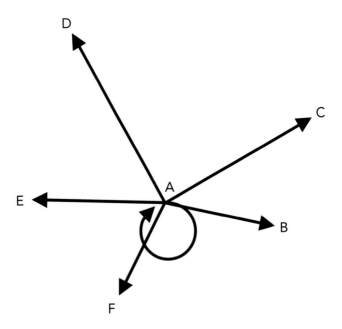

– 1 –

The Myth of the Genius

TRADITIONALLY, the process of conceiving design ideas is assumed to be an exclusively human activity. The common belief is that design is associated with purpose, intention, or aim and so it can only arise from the mind of a conscious designer. Terms such as preference, decision, action, or even more mundane ones, such as choice, assumption, mistake, or appearance, all involve an elementary level of consciousness, which only human beings can possess. The Chinese room paradox, posed by Searle in his paper "Minds, Brains, and Programs",[1] is an argument about intentionality, understanding, and conscious experience. It suggests a table in a room with cards depicting Chinese symbols and a set of rules on how to place them. A non-Chinese speaker enters the room and arranges the cards. Then a Chinese speaker enters the room, looks at the card arrangement, and claims that it is a delightful poem. Of course, the first person did not have the faintest idea of what he or she was doing and the effect that it would have. According to Searle, only humans possess the causal powers that give them intentionality, a necessary condition of thinking; otherwise it is only a metaphorical attribution.

One of the intrinsic characteristics of the practice of design is its reliance on ideas that are conceived, generated, or formed within the mind of a lead designer that are then propagated down the corporate ladder to be implemented, executed, or constructed by members of the design office. A human designer is always exclusively responsible for the conceptualization, creation, and control of ideas and in some design fields, such as architecture, this mental process is regarded as a particular, irreplaceable, and almost "sacred" privilege of the human mind that identifies, distinguishes, and celebrates the uniqueness of certain individuals. It is about the ability of certain architects to resolve programmatic complexity while addressing aesthetical, structural, sustainable, social, or even psychological issues all at the same time. Such an extraordinary ability is perceived by many as a supernatural one that leads occasionally to a mystifying admiration and celebrity status. Yet, it should be mentioned here that such supernatural abilities are witnessed and assumed only on the basis of the resulting products (i.e. the finished buildings), and very little is being reported, recorded, or revealed and therefore known about the process itself. Most of the evidence is based on retrospective monographs, metaphors, recollections, or sketches, the value, accuracy, or relevance of which can be questionable. Nonetheless, it is clear that architectural design offices do not work alone in confronting complexity during the design process but rather cooperatively with multiple engineers, scientists, sociologists, and other expert consultants and the resulting buildings are hardly the work of one individual but rather the accomplishment of a team.

The idea of a "genius" originated as a humanistic attempt to explain remarkable creative and original work on the basis of an exceptional natural intellectual capacity possessed by certain "gifted" individuals. It is an idea rooted into the Enlightenment that meant to point out, exert, and elevate human individuality and originality. Specifically, Schopenhauer's or Kant's definitions of a genius[2] are both based on the notion of originality, i.e. one's ability to think unlike any of the other fellow peers. It can be argued therefore that the notion of being a genius apart from a mental state can be also seen as a social construct. The ability of an individual to solve complex problems or to be creative can be based (apart from personal ability) on various other external factors such as accident, luck, coincidence, or publicity. This possibility opens up a more interesting potential than has been previously possible under the humanistic definition. Rather than assuming that a genius-individual is unique and therefore irreplaceable, it may also be appropriate to consider the process followed by a so-called genius. Of course, this assumes that the process is traceable, identifiable, repeatable, and therefore independent of the particular agent that carries it out. In other words, a genius-like system would be able to re-enact the steps that a genius would have taken in order to solve/address the problem.

As discussed earlier in the Chinese room paradox, the problem of re-enacting, simulating, or replicating human thought is impossible by any agent that lacks consciousness. Consciousness is a necessary condition for human thought or, according to Searle, any kind of thought. The presence of consciousness is a presupposition for intentionality, i.e. the deliberate relationship between mental acts and the external world. Every mental phenomenon has some content and is directed to an object, the intentional object. So, for instance, "belief" as a mental state is related to the object "believed" since without that relationship there would be no mental phenomenon. However, this train of thought, albeit self-consistent, is also circular by definition: intentionality is that which defines the mental and mental is that which is intentional. So, a question arises necessarily on whether something is thinkable because we can think of it or we can think of something because it is thinkable. The answer to this question can be viewed in at least two possible ways: either that thinking is a humanly initiated mechanism that requires for its validity consciousness or that thinking is simply the result of a mechanism, regardless of how or who produced it. The second option (a behaviorist one) implies that if something acts as if it is thinking, then it is thinking (until proof of the opposite). In such a case, the Turing test would be one way of distinguishing and defining such a thinking process not from its appearance or its intrinsic qualities but rather from its resulting behavior. So, in that sense, a genius will be defined as a genius not because it is human but rather because it behaves like a genius.

A computer is not human and therefore cannot think, let alone be a genius. Computer programs are sequences of instructions to be executed by a computer. The instructions are conceived by a human programmer and they abide by a series of grammatical and syntactical constraints also defined by other human programmers. The languages used by programmers are also defined by human programmers and engineers. In itself a computer program is simply a flow of electrons that is initiated, controlled, and interpreted by human beings. There is no consciousness or intentionality intricate or superimposed on or in a computer, which is also a machine constructed by human engineers. Intentionality, as defined by observing human behavior, is not only absent but also, by definition, impossible to exist within a computer. Any mechanism capable of producing intentionality must have causal relationships equal to those of the human brain. Instantiating a computer program is never by itself a sufficient condition of intentionality. Nevertheless, computer programs can be regarded as extensions of the human mind and as such they can inform, reveal, or extend the awareness of a human mind affecting the consciousness of humans. By taking advantage of the speed, efficiency, and quantity of logic-arithmetic operations, possibilities can be explored that are incapable or unpredictable to the human mind's intellectual ability.

Through the use of computation, knowledge can be acquired that is impossible or foreign to the human mind. There are two terms that need to be defined here first: impossible and foreign. Impossible refers to the inability to predict a result due to a large number of calculations. Foreign refers to the inability to comprehend the results of such calculations. For example, the solution or visualization of a recursive equation (e.g. a quadratic polynomial) may reveal behaviors unpredictable and often unexplainable, yet true. The assertion of truth is based on the rational structure of computational schemes and their consequent characteristic of being coherent, traceable, and consistent. It is assumed here that intelligence, as a rational process of problem solving, is not an exclusive privilege of the human mind but rather can be abstracted as a generalized process, codified in the form of rules, and then re-implemented into another medium, i.e. binary, chemical, biological, etc. In other words, human intelligence is a biological instantiation of a more general structure that manifests itself in what we define as "intelligence". Further, the implementation into an alternative medium takes advantage of the properties of that medium rendering results much faster, accurate, or complex. Most importantly, a human is able to compare one's own process with another non-human as to detect similarities or differences in performance, but also to engage in mutual or parallel synergy as to share, complement, and enhance either process.

While the computational mechanisms themselves are not conscious of the operations performed within their domain, yet the resulting computations often reveal schemes that are neither predictable nor understood by the humans who initiated them. Nonetheless, these schemes while intellectual are not dependent on human interpretation. For instance, recursive polynomial functions are the mathematical basis of fractal schemes, the behavior of which is revealed through computational operations. Yet, these fractal schemes are not dependent on human interpretations but rather are mechanisms implemented and observed in nature. The paradox here is that human consciousness is affected by intellectual schemes developed by machines that possess no consciousness. In contrast to material patterns formed by mechanical tools which serve as extensions to the human body, computational patterns have built into them logical and arithmetic structures neither of which are human inventions but rather discoveries of pre-existing mechanisms.

In the field of design, computational tools have been used quite extensively mainly as means for facilitating tedious graphical tasks but also as means for exploring formal patterns and behaviors. Various tasks in the design process have been replaced by computational tools liberating the designer from lengthy, repetitive, or difficult matters. Some of these tools are associated with the computer screen and its ability to temporarily shift or alter visual appearances. The illusion of motion, for instance, can be addressed by toggling consecutive pixels producing visual phenomena observed as "dragging" or "rubber-banding". Such alterations of pixel-based displays have an enormous effect and affect in the presentation, organization, but most importantly in the conceptualization of design. The interaction of the designer with the phenomena produced on their computer screens has become a main topic of interest in the recent literature surrounding computer-aided design. While this interaction does have a profound effect on the designer's consciousness, the role of the computer is identified merely as that of an aid, assistant, or medium even though the processes followed by the computer may be identical to those of a human except for the computer's lack of consciousness and intentionality.

The idea of design as deriving from the mind of a conscious designer has been affected significantly by computational tools occasionally blurring the distinction between what the designer originally wanted and what the designer eventually did. It is quite common for designers to end up with formal solutions that are not only entirely different to hand-drawn ones but also stylistically similar when using the same software. It can be argued that no matter how creative one can be, the use of any CAD modeling program will significantly reduce the possible solutions, expressions, and presentations that one can have and therefore result in a "tool mannerism".

Yet, this discrepancy between what was intended and what was produced is not compatible with mechanical means and their effect on design conceptualization. There, mechanical forces produce material patterns that have an affect on the designer's interpretation. For instance, pen–paper physical interaction, color filters on a camera, or yellow trace layering are mechanical actions with material effects that get interpreted by humans in various ways. The difference between such effects and those produced by a computer is in the intellectual nature of the second. The term intellectual is used here, rather narrowly, as the capacity for rational or intelligent activity intrinsic to the agent that displays it. In contrast to a mechanical behavior, which is determined mainly by physical or chemical interactions, a computational event involves logical and arithmetic operations that are intrinsic to the behavior exhibited. In other words, a mechanical tool is a physical entity with a behavior dependent on the user's will whereas a computational tool is the result of a logical process that determines its behavior. For example, a pen is a physical entity with a behavior dependent on the writer's will whereas a pixel leaving a trace on a computer screen is the result of a logical process that involves logical interactions between neighboring pixels placed on a grid. Ultimately, both tools are developed by human tool makers and both events are interpreted by the human designer who gets ideas based on one's conscious observations.

The problem with consciousness when it is applied to the process of design is in the interdependency of their definitions. If a design is the result of a conscious decision, then, of course, consciousness is a necessary condition for design. In that sense, by definition anything non-conscious cannot design. However, the problem here is that both definitions are taken from the human's viewpoint; that is, design and conscious are seen as verbs not nouns. As verbs both terms are immediately associated with action and therefore with intentionality. But if they are seen as nouns then their value lies within their own existence and the observer's role is to confirm their value, not to determine it. The possibility of such a distinction opens up a more intricate relationship for viewing design than has been previously possible. Rather than assuming the presence of a conscious designer, instead design can be seen as a phenomenon regardless of its creator. In that context, the terms "conscious" and "design" need to be re-identified, distinguished, and perhaps redefined in the light of their own existence.

Consciousness and intentionality are two terms that can be contrasted to those of randomness and contradiction. A conscious person cannot be random even if one intends to be so because that would contradict the very premise upon which consciousness is based: controlled thought. Randomness by definition is connected to the lack of control over the outcome of a process. While apprehension of randomness as an external phenomenon is possible by a conscious observer the mere inability to predict the outcome defines it as random by that same observer. Similarly, contradiction is by definition antithetical to intentionality. One cannot be intentionally contradictory because that would negate the very nature of intentionality, which is consistency. Of course, one can say so (i.e. that "I intend to be contradictory") but that is just a phrase, a series of words in a sentence, not a consistent and truthful argument.

The explanatory power of rational thinking relies on the principles of consistency, coherency, and predictability, principles often considered antithetical to those of contradiction, paradox, or randomness. While the former principles have an established value within the Western philosophical tradition as being the only means by which truth can be explored, extracted, and established, the latter principles are also widely used except not scientifically but rather in the form of poetry, myth, or story-telling. In those cases, consistency is not the main focus as there is no outcome that needs to be proven but rather the text itself serves as a platform for the reader to interpret the meanings presented to without any definite, traceable, or provable purpose. Nevertheless, there is a great difference between nonsense and contradiction: just because a thought may contain two antithetical notions does not render it also as incomprehensible. In fact, the very notion of antithesis itself involves the coexistence of contrasting notions not in the sense of comparison to a perfect reference but rather as a balance between forces, the nature of which may not even be known.

The difference between consistency and contradiction is not only in the methods but also in the premises of the argument: namely its definition. A definition is a point of reference, a starting point. The clarity of a definition is an essential part of a proof since it is impossible to prove something when one does not know what it is. However, the problem of a definition is that it is based on existing knowledge; that is, on information upon which there is common agreement. The problem with this definition of definition is that not all things can be described accurately in order to convey their fundamental meaning. Most importantly, a definition is a human construction made to serve the means of communication and common agreement in order to establish a basis for consistency and it is not indicative of the nature of the term. In other words, a definition is intrinsically associated with the people who agree with it. If there is no one to articulate a definition of something and no one to agree with it then there is no definition. Yet, that does not mean that this something does not exist. In fact, almost anything existed before it was defined. A definition serves only the purpose of human communication and is in no way an ontological establishment.

A computer program that uses randomness as a means to address a problem is very different from a computer program that follows the instructions of a programmer to address the same program. In the second case, the program is a mirror of the thoughts and intentions of the programmer, whereas in the first case the programmer is unaware of the solution strategy despite his or her intentional typing up, initiating, or running the program on a machine that is also constructed by humans. Randomness, as established earlier, is a disassociation of one's intentions and therefore does not follow the principles of rational human thinking, i.e. consistency, coherency, and predictability. Nevertheless, the results of a random process may be revealing of a way that things work and therefore can be used by the user to address the problem. The gap between what a programmer intended to do and what they actually did is indeed a human interpretation but the gap itself is not. The gap itself is a glimpse into a possibility unknown to us through a process also unknown to us. After the fact, a definition may be established that will add to human knowledge and become a point of reference or a definition for agreement among humans in the future.

In the world of design, computer programs have taken over many traditionally human intellectual tasks leaving fewer and fewer tasks for traditional designers to do. From Photoshop filters to modeling applications and from simulation programs to virtual reality animation and even more mundane tasks that used to need a certain talent to take on, such as rendering, paper cutting, or 3D sculpting, the list of tasks diminishes day by day only to be replaced by their computational counterparts. What used to be a basis to judge somebody as a talent or a genius is no longer applicable. Dexterity, adeptness, memorization, fast calculation, or aptitude are no longer skills to look for in a designer or reasons to admire a designer as to be called a genius. The focus has shifted far away from what it used to be toward new territories. In the process many take advantage of the ephemeral awe that the new computational tools bring to design by using them as means to establish a new concept or form only to be revealed later that their power was based on the tool they used and not on their own intellectual ability. After all, the tool was developed by somebody else, the programmer who discovered the tool's mechanism, and should, perhaps, be considered instead the innovator.

As a result of the use and abuse of design tools, many have started to worry about the direction that design will take in the next few years. As one by one all design tasks are becoming computational, some regard this as a danger, misfortune, or inappropriation of what design should be and others as a liberation, freedom, and power toward what design should be, i.e. conceptualization. According to the latter, the designer does not need to worry any more about the construction documents, schedules, databases, modeling, rendering, animation, etc. and can now concentrate on what is most important: the concept. But what if that is also replaced?

What if one day a new piece of software appears that allows one to input the building program and then produces valid designs, i.e. plan, elevation, and sections that work? And, worse, what if they are better than the designer would have ever done by himself or herself? (Even though most designers would never admit publicly that something is better than what they would have designed, yet what if deep inside them they would admit the opposite?) What then? Are we still going to continue demonizing the computer and seeking to promote geniuses when they really don't exist?

If that ever happens, then obviously the focus of design will not be in the process itself since that can be replaced but rather in the replacement operation itself. The new designer will construct the tool that will enable one to design in an indirect meta-design way. As the current condition indicates, the original design is laid out in the computer program that addresses the issues not in the mind of the user. If the tool maker and the tool user is the same person then intentionality and randomness can coexist within the same system and the gap can be bridged. Maybe then the solution to the Chinese room paradox is not inside or outside the room but rather in the passage that connects the two.

More than ever now because of the dependency on technology in contemporary design practice the problem of consciousness and intentionality has raised critical questions of identity, authenticity, or responsibility at least on the side of the designer. Who is the designer today and how important are one's own ideas versus the techniques provided in an increasingly digitally dominated world? It may be claimed that the use of digital technologies in design, as well as in everyday activities, has deep and profound consequences not only in the way thoughts and ideas are conceived, understood, and communicated but also in their intrinsic value and validity. Is it possible to design without a computer today? Is it that digital techniques have become determinant conditions, perhaps hidden, upon which the designers, practitioners, or critics base their ideas, thoughts, or even ideologies? How important it is for designers to know the mechanisms of software or hardware and therefore the limits that these technologies impose on design and does that even matter any more?

Today, computers are increasingly involved in the design process. Their roles vary from drafting and modeling to intelligent knowledge-based processing of architectural information. While the future of computers appears to include a variety of possible roles, it is worth exploring these roles in the context provided by the question: "Who designs?" If one takes the position that designing is not exclusively a human activity and that ideas exist independently of human beings, then it would be possible to design a computer mechanism that relates ideas.

Rational thinking, regardless of whether it applies to humans or machines, relies on the principles of consistency, coherency, and predictability, principles often considered antithetical to those of contradiction, paradox, or conflict. While the former principles have an established value within the Western philosophical tradition as being the only means by which truth can be extracted, tested, and established, the latter principles are also widely used in Western thought except not scientifically but rather in the form of poetry, myth, or story-telling. In those cases, consistency is not the main focus as there is no outcome that needs to be proven but rather the text itself serves as a metaphor, allegory, or allusion, inviting the reader to interpret the meanings alluded to without any definite, traceable, or provable purpose. A poem, for instance, is not about a conclusion, an outcome, or a proof, but rather about the narration itself even if it contains contradictions, doubts, or polemics. Nevertheless, there is a great difference between nonsense and contradiction: just because a thought may contain two antithetical notions that does not render it also as incomprehensible. In fact, the very notion of antithesis itself involves the coexistence of contrasting notions not in the sense of comparison to a perfect reference but rather as a balance between forces, the nature of which may not even be known. For instance, the concept of a road can be defined as a path that connects points A and B but also as the coexistence of two directions (left and right or up and down). In that sense, the statement "the way up is also the way down" contrasts two opposite notions within the same term establishing a contradiction. But unlike being an inconsistent contradiction (i.e. nonsense) this one involves an antithesis, the meaning of which is acquired through a complementary coupling of contrasting notions. It may be argued that the meaning of the pair is established through unification rather than addition or comparison.

The difference between consistency and contradiction is not only in the methods but also in the premises of the argument: namely its definition. A definition is a point of reference, a starting point. The clarity of a definition is an essential part of a proof since it is impossible to prove something when one does not know what it is. However, the problem of a definition is that it is based on existing knowledge; that is, on information upon which there is common agreement. The problem with this definition (or rather, this definition of definition) is that not all things can be described accurately in order to convey their fundamental meaning. Consider the possibility that there may be notions that cannot be described but nevertheless can be understood in a non-consequential non-descriptive manner. Take, for instance, the notion of complexity.

Complexity is a term used to denote the length of a description of a system or the amount of time required to create a system.[3] From networks and computers to machines and buildings there is a great deal of effort spent on how to understand, explain, model, or design systems whose scope, scale, and complexity often challenge the ability of designers to fully comprehend them. While complexity may be a characteristic of many systems or processes in nature, within the field of design the study of complexity is associated with artificial, synthetic, and human-made systems. Such systems, despite being human creations, consist of parts and relationships arranged in such complicated ways that often surpass a single designer's ability to thoroughly comprehend them even if that person is their own creator. Paradoxical as it may appear, humans today have become capable of exceeding their own intellect. Through the use of advanced computer systems, intricate algorithms, and massive computations, designers are able to extend their thoughts into a once unknown and unimaginable world of complexity. Yet, it may be argued that the inability of the human mind to single-handedly grasp, explain, or predict artificial complexity is caused mainly by quantitative constraints; that is, by the *amount* of information or the *time* it takes to compute it and not necessarily on the intellectual ability of humans to comprehend, infer, or reason about such complexities. Nevertheless, while this assumption may be true, it is only so because of the lack of any other explanation. In other words, if humans are not aware of artificial complexity then who is? After all, artificial is by definition human and so are its resulting complexities. However, there is a special category of complexity that even though human-made is not only unpredictable, incomprehensible, or inconceivable by humans but also strange, foreign, and unfamiliar: randomness.

Randomness is a term used to describe a lack of an identifiable pattern, purpose, or objective. In its formal manifestation, randomness can also be defined as a meaningless pattern. While this definition can be applied to the description of a pattern being random, it becomes problematic when it is applied to the act of creating a random pattern. The claim itself involves a self-referential paradox: how can one create something that is meaningless? Wouldn't the mere act of creation itself assign meaning automatically? In other words, randomness is the process of creating no meaning, which is a contradictory claim. Let's consider the following sentence: "This statement is meaningless." If it is, then its meaning is that it is meaningless and if it is not, then it has a meaning. This logical paradox is referred to as a self-referential, "begging the question", or circular fallacy because the premises of the argument include the claim that the conclusion is true. In other words, the creation of randomness involves intention, which is contrary to randomness. However peculiar this may sound, by definition one cannot create randomness. The moment one makes a random move it ceases to be random because it can be interpreted later as a series of causal steps. Nevertheless, while one may not be able to create randomness on one's own will, one can certainly witness it by observing others. That is, if another person makes a move unpredictable to the first person then that move is random for as long as the first person cannot identify a pattern, purpose, or objective.

Complexity, as defined earlier, is associated with randomness in the following way: if a pattern is very regular, it is easy to describe, and so it is simple. In contrast, if it is irregular, then it is difficult to describe, and so it becomes complex. If it is so complex that the information it contains cannot be compressed at all, we say that it is random. So randomness is characterized as the maximum of complexity, and as the opposite of regularity and simplicity. Consider the following binary sequences A and B:

A: 00100100100100100100100100100100100100100100100100100 . . .
B: 10110100110100100100111010101011110010001000011001101011 . . .

Apparently, the first sequence is a repetition of 001 whereas the second one does not appear to have any identifiable pattern that can be further compressed and so it will be assumed to be random until proof of the opposite. Now, consider the following sentence A and a random rearrangement of the words in the sentence B:

A: if it exists, you can think of it
B: if you can think of it, it exists

While preserving the grammatical and syntactical correctness, a random shift in the sequence of words in the sentence A produces a sentence B very different from the original sentence A.

In this case, randomness functions as a transformation from one state into another producing a new form from an existing one. This structural behavior resembles in many ways Dadaist poetry, or Marcov processes. In those cases, an algorithm functions as a string rewriting system that uses grammar-like rules to operate on strings of symbols in order to generate new strings of text. While the syntax of the resulting text may be consistent with the grammatical rules, the meaning of the resulting text is not necessarily associated semantically to the intentions of the original code. In those cases, the introduction of randomness in the arrangement of text can produce results that are unpredictable, complicated, but also accidentally meaningful. Yet, just because something is random does not necessitate that it is also unpredictable. Unpredictability is, by definition, a disassociation of intention. But unlike chaos, a random rearrangement of elements within a rule-based system produces effects that even though unpredictable are intrinsically connected through the rules that govern that system. In a similar, almost humorous fashion, the Dadaist engine is a computer algorithm that produces random text based on a recursive rearrangement of elements in a grammar. The resulting text, while allegedly based on random processes, is readable, occasionally it makes sense, and in some cases the text is surprisingly intelligent. While in all of these cases it is quite apparent that awareness, consciousness, or intention is missing, the resulting language patterns are convincing enough to "fool" someone to believe that they were authentic; that is, worthy of trust, reliance, or belief, as if they were produced by a sentient author. In one case, a paper constructed using the Dada Engine software was allegedly almost admitted to a conference, which, had it happened would have passed Turing's classic test of computer intelligence.

In the field of design, similarities may exist on formal, visual, or structural levels. Computational rearrangement of formal rules that describe, define, and formulate a certain style can produce a permutation of possible formal expressions for that style. For instance, drawing on Andrea Palladio's original forty-odd designs of villas, Hersey and Freedman were able to detect, extract, and formulate rigorous geometric rules by which Palladio conceived these structures. Using a computational algorithm, they were able to create villa plans and facades that are stylistically indistinguishable from those of Palladio himself. Similarly, Dannenberg and Shusta developed an algorithm that produces all possible combinations of skyscrapers for a given site (see Figure 1.1). Their strategy involves physical and geometric parameters to script a computer modeling code that builds, renders, and organizes an infinite number of skyscraper possibilities, from which emerges a formal pedigree categorized in texture and performance. What is remarkable about this – or any other combinatorial analysis – is that they are able to produce computationally any possible form ever created or any yet to be created.

Algorithms can be used to solve, organize, or explore problems with increased visual or organizational complexity. In its simplest form, a computational algorithm uses numerical methods to address problems. The basic linguistic elements used in algorithms are constants, variables, procedures, classes, and libraries and the basic operations are arithmetical, logical, combinatorial, relational, and classificatory arranged under specific grammatical and syntactical rules. These elements and operations are designed to address the numerical nature of computers while at the same time providing the means for composing logical patterns. However, while numbers are often regarded as discrete quantitative units that are utilized for measuring, yet in computational terms numbers can be constructed that can address an infinite degree of division thus exhibiting theoretical continuity. Similarly, random variables or conditions can be inserted in an algorithm further increasing the degree of unpredictability of the final outcome and magnifying the level of complexity. Contrary to common belief, algorithms are not only deterministic processes developed to explain, reason, or predict a humanly conceived problem but rather can become venues for addressing complexities that exceed a human's ability to explain, reason, or predict.

The random application of rules on a random pattern does not necessarily produce further randomness but surprisingly may produce a certain degree of order. Buffon's experiment with needles[4] showed that random sampling contributes to a stochastic approximation of the number $[N] = 3.141592\ldots$ In a similar fashion, random application of simple rules on random patterns produces a phenomenon referred to as self-organization. Self-organization is the progressive development of a system out of a random initial condition into an organized form. Instead of applying a center-based hierarchical decision-making process to create order, we use a parallel multiple decision-making process based on local neighboring information that contributes toward a collective emergent ordered behavior. In such systems, called cellular automata,[5] local agents interact with one another based on rules pertinent to the information at their level and contribute information synchronically toward a collective decision that often exhibits unexpected behavior, such as that of self-organization. Such systems exhibit autonomy, self-maintenance, adaptation, heterogeneity, complexity, and order. Cellular automata have been used to describe, explain, and predict complex behaviors exhibited in biology, mathematics, physics, or social systems.

An alternative approach to cellular automata, called a genetic or evolutionary algorithm,[6] is based on evolutionary biology, using terms and processes such as genomes, chromosomes, cross-over, mutation, or selection. The evolution starts from a population of completely random individuals and happens in generations. In each generation, the fitness of the whole population is evaluated, multiple individuals are stochastically selected from the current population (based on their fitness), modified (mutated or recombined) to form a new population, which becomes current in the next iteration of the algorithm. Such systems lead to the emergence of ordered patterns that can simulate, explain, and predict complex behaviors. Random patterns are iteratively enhanced and evaluated until a set of satisfying conditions is met. Genetic algorithms solve local neighborhood behavior and then move further to resolve global, to the system, issues. In that way there is an emergent behavior embedded in the process of deriving possible solutions to a problem. This behavior is based on the premise that individual units under certain constraints may emerge into globally functional configurations by resolving their local neighboring conditions in a repetitive manner. Contrary to common belief such seemingly chaotic local behavior does not necessarily result into chaotic overall behavior, but rather into an evolved form that optimizes (if not resolves) the local constraints.

One of the main problems in architecture today is the quantity of the information and the level of complexity involved in most building projects, especially in high rises and

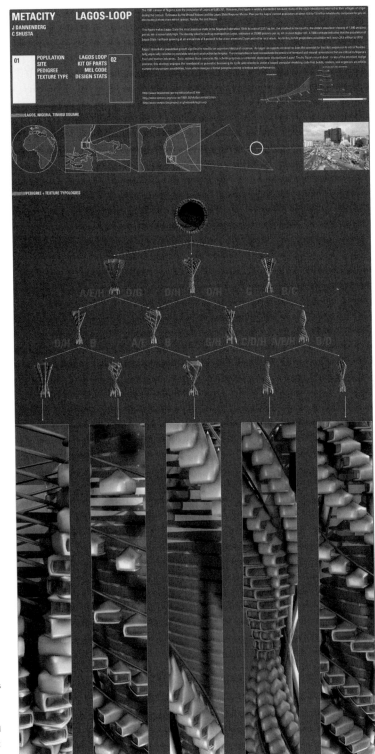

1.1 Skyscraper studies using combinatorial analysis (project by Joshua Dannenberg and Chris Shusta for course GSD 2311 taught by Kostas Terzidis at Harvard University)

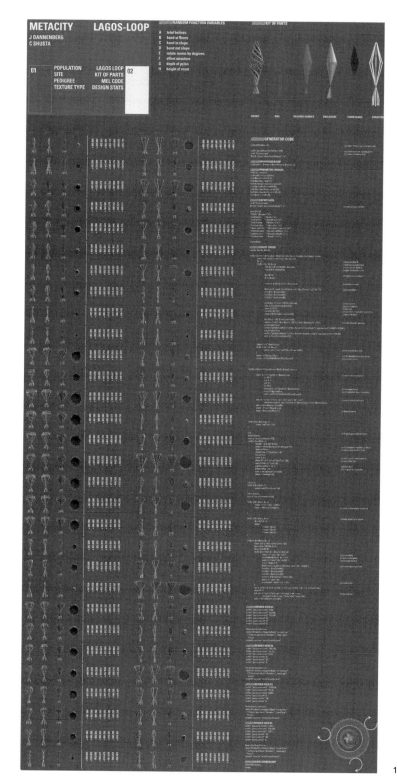

1.1 continued

large-scale housing projects. Housing projects for a few hundred to thousands of people have started to emerge over large urban areas. In such cases, the old paradigm for housing design was the development of high rises that served as stacking devices for multiple family housing units. Such a direction is unfortunately the only way to address excessive complexity using manual design skills mainly because it is simple to conceive but also simple to construct. The unfortunate nature of this approach lies rather in the uniformity, similarity, and invariability that these projects express in comparison to individuality, discreteness, and identity that human beings and families express. In these projects there is a typology of residential units that need to be combined in various schemes that will fulfill multiple functional, environmental, and economic constraints. While small apartment buildings may be solvable within one architect's design capabilities, the design and planning of large projects with several thousand inhabitants is a challenge. The problem is to fulfill all complex requirements without using conventional repetitive high-rise patterns. Snyder and Ding addressed the problem of large-scale high-rise housing by using cellular automata as an ordering device to fulfill multiple housing constraints (see Figure 1.2). Similarly, Somnez and Bu used stochastic search to determine the position of building elements within a high rise (see Figure 1.3).

What makes randomness problematic for designers and architects is that they have traditionally maintained the view that design is associated with purpose, intention, or aim. Design is thus contrasted with purposelessness, randomness, or lack of complexity. The traditional view is that design can only arise out of the mind of a sentient designer. Challenging these assumptions computational theories have proposed an alternative definition of design, in which it is still meaningful to speak of design without always speaking of a sentient designer. Rather than assuming the presence of a sensible mind, it may be that certain impersonal forces are equally capable of giving rise to a phenomenon called design. These two antithetical positions, albeit metaphysical, present two different theoretical approaches to the intellectual origin of design.

Within the emergence of digital processes, it can be argued that certain qualities of the human mind such as those that contribute to what is considered "smart" (i.e. sharpness, quick thought, or brightness) may not be desirable or even applicable when dealing with the computer's reasoning. What is considered to be smart in the one world may be considered dumb in the other world.[7] Traditionally, the dominant mode for discussing creativity in architecture has always been that of intuition and talent, where stylistic ideas are pervaded by an individual, a genius, or a group of talented partners within a practice. In contrast, an algorithm is a procedure, the result of which is not necessarily credited to its creator. Algorithms are understood as abstract and universal mathematical operations that can be applied to almost any kind or any quantity of elements. It is not about the person who invented it but rather about its efficiency, speed, and generality. It can be argued therefore that human decision making (i.e. manual design) can be arbitrary, authoritative, and, often, naive in comparison to computational schemes where complexity, consistency, and generality are celebrated liberating design from subjective interpretations and leading toward the emergence of designs that while functional may surprise even their own creators. These two distinct practices have deep and profound differences that are both ideological and methodological.

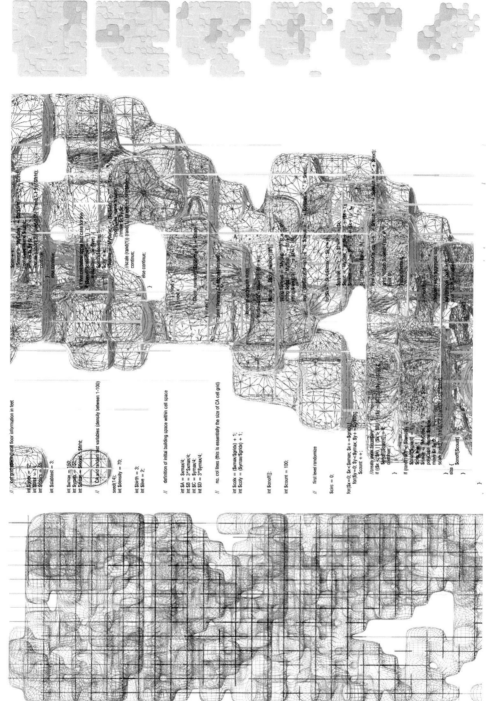

1.2 Large-scale housing project using cellular automata (project by Mathew Snyder and Jeff Ding for course GSD 2311 taught by Kostas Terzidis at Harvard University)

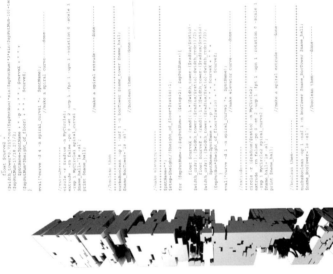

1.3 Skyscraper studies using stochastic search and random sampling (project by Mete Sonmez and XiaoJun Bu for course GSD 2311 taught by Kostas Terzidis at Harvard University)

For the last four decades, beginning with Christopher Alexander's *Notes of the Synthesis of Form* and Robert Venturi's *Complexity and Contradiction in Architecture* and continuing through a plethora of formal studies and computational methods,[8] designers, architects, and urban planners have been primarily concerned with increased complexity involved in the design of buildings, urban areas, and cities. Research and professional practice have attempted to automate traditional "manual" methods of production using computer-aided design tools and to consider architectural schools and offices as hubs for cross-pollination among diverse engineering disciplines. When comparing architectural design and other software-intensive engineering design disciplines it is necessary to overlook many significant and distinguishing differences in order to identify at least one common theme: the use of computational methods to address excessively complex tasks.

Historically, algorithms have been used quite extensively in architecture. While the connotation of an algorithm may be associated with the science of computers, nonetheless the use of instructions, commands, or rules in architectural practice are, in essence, algorithms. Architectural design has also a long history of addressing complex programmatic requirements through a series of steps yet without a specific design target. Unlike other design fields where the target is to solve a particular problem in the best possible way, architectural design is open-ended, flux, and uncertain. Codified information, such as standards, codes, specifications, or types, simply serve the purpose of conforming to functional requirements, yet are not guarantees for a successful design solution. However, while deciding under uncertainty requires some degree of experience, intuition, and ingenuity it may be also argued that it requires an ability to make as many random mistakes as it takes until an acceptable solution is encountered. Traditionally, the second requirement, while plausible, has never been considered as a viable option for at least two reasons: because it is simply too hard to go through all the possibilities that exist, but, most importantly, because it lacks the most important ingredient of any decision: human involvement. A decision is by definition intentional, and therefore human. Computational systems lack causal powers that would give them intentionality, a necessary condition of thinking. Terms such as understanding, deciding, responding, or even more mundane ones such as knowing, suggesting, or helping, involve an elementary level of consciousness, which computational devices do not possess. And yet, paradoxically, such systems occasionally do come up with interesting solutions using random iterations, which are characterized by the use of dubious names such as genetic, artificial, or automatic, none of which is theoretically accurate.

Because of its quantitative nature, the study of complexity involves by necessity computational methods as means of analysis, simulation, and synthesis of systems that involve large amounts of information or information processing. Unlike traditional methods of analysis and synthesis, computational schemes offer a degree of rationality that allows them to migrate into computer-executable programs. Further, the ability to produce large amounts of random sampling allows explorations of multiple solutions some of which may have never been conceived by the designer. Such a possibility opens up enormous potential than has been previously possible; rather than utilizing mere human-based intelligence in resolving design problems, a complementary synergetic relationship between humans and computers becomes possible. Therefore, any scientific approach to design needs to take into consideration not only systematic, methodical, and rational models, but also alternative approaches that address the nature of design as an indefinite, ill-defined, and chaotic process.

Both architects and engineers argue for the deployment of computational strategies for addressing, resolving, and satisfying complicated design requirements. These strategies result from a logic, which is based on the premise that systematic, methodical, and traceable patterns of thought are capable of resolving almost any design problem. While this assumption may be true for well-defined problems, most design problems are not always clearly defined. In fact, the notion of design as an abstract, ambiguous, indefinite, and unpredictable intellectual phenomenon is quite attuned to the very nature of the definition – or perhaps lack of – a single definition of design. Yet, the mere existence of certain ambiguous qualities such as indefiniteness, vagueness, or elusiveness serve as indications that perhaps design is not only about an epiphany, the extraordinary intellectual power of a genius, or a methodical collage of construction elements but also a progressive optimizing search for possible solutions based on iterative random sampling. While the second approach may sound foreign, naive, or even dangerous to some, it does possess a certain degree of merit due to its practical implementations within a progressively computational design world. Indeed, the philosophical implications are even more interesting as they challenge the very nature of what design is, or even further, what creating is. Nevertheless, regardless of the intrinsic differences it is clear that both positions are essential in detecting, understanding, and addressing design complexity.

Notes

1. Searle, John, "Minds, Brains and Programs", *Behavioral and Brain Sciences*, vol. 3, 1980, pp. 417–57.

2. See Kant, I., *The Critique of Judgment* (Section 46) and Schopenhauer, A., *The Art of Literature* (Chapter: On Style).

3. This definition, also referred to as Kolmogorov's or K-complexity, offers a distinction between visual and structural complexity. Regardless of the complexity involved in the appearance of a pattern, by definition complexity is based on the reproducing algorithm; that is, a series of instructions that will regenerate the visual pattern.

4. Georges-Louis Leclerc, Comte de Buffon, in the eighteenth century, noticed that the probability of randomly thrown needles to lie across lines on a floor made of parallel strips of wood approximates [N].

5. See von Neumann, John, *The Theory of Self-reproducing Automata*, A. Burks, ed., Urbana, IL: University of Illinois Press, 1966.

6. See Holland, John H., Genetic Algorithms: Computer programs that "evolve" in ways that resemble natural selection can solve complex problems even their creators do not fully understand, *Scientific American*, 1992.

7. For instance, to find a secret password a human may exploit context-based conjectures, reductive reasoning, or assumptions as strategies for saving time and effort. In contrast, a computer can solve the same problem by simply checking all possible combinations of all alphanumeric symbols until a match is found. Such a strategy, referred to as brute force, would be considered overwhelming, pointless, naive, or impossible by a human investigator.

Nonetheless, given the computational power of a computer, such a "strategy" may only take a few seconds to check millions of possibilities, something inconceivable to the human mind.

8. See Alexander, C., *Notes on the Synthesis of Form*, Cambridge, MA: Harvard University Press, 1967, and Venturi, C., *Complexity and Contradiction in Architecture* (2nd edn), New York: Museum of Modern Art, 2002; also see Novak, M., "Computational Compositions", *ACADIA 88 Proceedings*, pp. 5–30, Mitchell, W., *Logic of Architecture*, Cambridge, MA: MIT Press, 1990, and Eisenmann, P., "Visions Unfolding: Architecture In The Age Of Electronic Media", *Intelligente Ambiente, Ars Eletronica*, 1992, Frazer, J., *An Evolutionary Architecture*, London: Architectural Association, 1995, and Lynn, Greg, *Animate Form*, New York: Princeton Architectural Press, 1999.

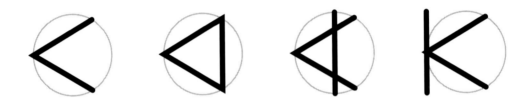

– 2 –

Parasight(s)

A parasite is an organism that lives through, on, or in another organism, which is called a host. In some cases, it is a natural symbiotic relationship between two organisms, the result of which is the sharing of common resources for mutual benefit. A common characteristic of a parasitical relationship is the balanced reliance on one another. Typically though, it is possible that the balance may be tilted at the expense of the host resulting in deterioration, destruction, or ultimately death. As a result, both organisms perish. However, there are cases in which the parasite does not perish after the death of the host but instead continues to feed from the dead body for a period of time and then migrates to another host.

A parasitical relationship, while observed as a natural relationship inhibiting living organisms, may be also used as a metaphor for describing abstract relationships between abstract entities. In such a case, something can be depended on something else in such a way so that the relationship appears ambiguous: when seen from the host's point of view it appears as if the host and the parasite both perished. But when seen from the parasite's point of view it appears as if the host is simply only a fertile ground for the continuous livelihood of the parasite. The picture of a dead grasshopper inhabited by mushroom plants that pollinate into other living grasshoppers is an instance of such an ambiguous relationship. The grasshoppers can be seen as an endless staircase upon which the mushroom seed proceeds.

A parasight is an intellectual idea that emerges through, on, or in the body of a theoretical structure by interpretation, mutation, and transgression. It is a hidden underlying intellectual scheme that feeds on the existing mode of thought. It serves as a means of alternative, foreign, or alien expressions that function as a critique to the existing intellectual status quo offering a reactive force against the overarching ideology. But a parasight is not a paradigm shift; at least not in the sense of Kuhn's definition of a paradigm shift. Because if it were, then it would have something in common with the paradigm from which it emerged, and thus, denying a completely radical change. Contrary to any paradigm shift, a parasight has a resemblance to the host body that allows it to be able to hide and stay dormant and undetected within its host body. A parasight may appear to have some resemblance to the previous ideological systems at a phenomenal level but that is so only because the interpreter thinks so based on the current knowledge. A parasight is an alien, foreign, and unfamiliar concept that, until understood, is interpreted as resembling something familiar. That doesn't mean that it is nonsensical, but in the absence of anything else to compare it with an interpreter will choose by definition the closest possible resemblance, either in the form of a comparison or of a metaphor.

A parasight defies a linguistic definition. In Wittgenstein's or Whorf's sense, the limits of language are the limits of the world. What we cannot think, we cannot say. Language cannot define the undefined: by definition. It can assign or construct a matching word but that does not define it in the true sense of the meaning. It is simply a circular definition, i.e. that which is not possible to be defined is defined as "undefined". However, we can assign a possibility that someday something undefined will be defined, but that is simply a wish and not a fact. Occasionally and regrettably, research or academic institutions take on subjects that, after extensive investigation, result in journal articles, papers, books, or reports, and in at the eyes of the public appear to be solved yet the subject of investigation is not complete. This leads to gaps in knowledge that lead to false assumptions, mistakes, and misinformation.

The word parasight is composed of the two parts: "para" and "sight". The word "sight" is, of course, English and it means vision, or the ability to see.[1] In this case, it signifies the ability to comprehend. But the word "para" is much more interesting. In its original Greek form it means any of the following: through, against, over, or instead. So, in that sense, a parasight is something that allows one to "see through, against, over, or instead".

A parasight is not human. Because if it were, then it would have to be conceived in or by someone and that means that at least one person would be responsible directly or indirectly for witnessing its existence. Human senses are limited to their physical means of acquiring signals from the material world. Similarly, human thought is limited not only in the information entered through the senses but also in its internal structure. There are limits of speed, capacity, and quantity of information stored or processed to name a few.

A parasight is logical, coherent, and consistent, and yet not understood. However, just because something is not understood does not mean that it defies logic. After all, if it were illogical we would not be able to understand it. In contrast, while logic is a method of understanding, it has limitations when applied to the human mind. Certain concepts are either too complicated or too unpredictable and so cannot be understood. Yet that does not mean that they are illogical, incoherent, or inconsistent. Simply, their logic is beyond the sphere of human apprehension and, until they are simplified, reduced, or decoded, they will remain non-understood.

The term parasight defers from but may be confused with the concept of a paradigm. A paradigm is an assumed way of thinking in the sense of being a generally accepted perspective of a particular discipline at a given time. Gradual changes in assumptions within a paradigm lead to a shift in meanings, understandings, or connotations. A parasight is different. It involves a drastic leap in reasoning in which a concept is formed on the basis of an apocalypse, epiphany, or revelation; that is, a rewiring of neural connections as to uncover a different path to a concept. Such a revelation can be of paramount importance as it opens a new set of possibilities for understanding, comprehending, and communicating but also for assimilating, filtering, and synthesizing new concepts.

Because of its seemingly incomprehensible and momentarily irrational behavior, a parasight is dismissed as a miscommunication as it questions the established expectations of what is referred to as "common sense". Common sense, in turn, is based on linguistic elements that have an established mapping between objects and symbols. Because of the "established" nature of such mappings little or none is referred to about the origin and history of the mappings. While such an "established" condition may be simple, practical, and useful, it may also intentionally or unintentionally hide, distract, or obscure the original or alternative mappings producing confusion, misunderstanding, or miscommunication. For instance, the English word for "a carved or cast figure of a person or an animal" (according to the *New Oxford American Dictionary*) is defined as a "statue" (also *statue* in French, *statua* in Italian, *estatua* in Spanish, and *Statue* in German). On a superficial level, such a definition justifies an apparently direct mapping between a word and an externally visible object. On an etymological level, the word "statue" itself is derived from the Latin word *statuere*,[2] which means "to stand up". So, conceptually, a statue must and should stand up; at least so that it justifies its definition. In Greek, however, the word statue is ΑΓΑΛΜΑ (prn agalma) derived from the verb ΑΓΑΛΛΩ (prn agalo), which means please, honor, or respect the Gods. There is no reference to the condition of standing up. Instead, a statue is that which pleases the Gods regardless of its posture, direction, or position. In fact, there is no reference to its shape, representation, and material consistency. It is possible to find Greek statues buried in the ground so nobody will ever see (except the Gods) or reliefs embedded into rock where the hidden part is equally curved with the same precision as the visible part but which nobody can see (except the Gods).[3]

Interestingly, while the words STATUE and ΑΓΑΛΜΑ are just a set of letters, they can also communicate a meaning as a whole word. Because of the semantic mapping between words and concepts, letters have lost their meaning as communication symbols in their own right. This predisposal to discern complex entities instead of simple ones is due to education, repetition, and habit. Challenging these assumptions, in other languages, such as Chinese, every symbol can be understood separately as a concept, but also, the combination of symbols into groups (i.e. words) is also understood as a separate concept. For example, 一 (prn Yi) is understood as "one" and 心 (prn xin) is understood as "heart". However, the combination of both into a word is 不 (prn bu) which, strangely enough, means "no" (that is, the negation of something). So, in this case, while two symbols are understood as separate meanings, the combination of them means something completely different. Or, the same sentence can be phrased as, "while a word is understood as something, its constituent elements can be understood as something completely different". However, it may also be that these differences may be phenomenal. By careful analysis of the constituent elements one may interpret the meaning of the word. So, in the case of 不, the two symbols are set in a vertical position, where 一 is up and 心 is below it. Now, 一 (e.g. one) can be interpreted as heaven and 心 (e.g. heart) can be interpreted as a free bird. In that case, the symbol 不 can also be interpreted as a "bird ascending to heaven". Which means "no". Why? Why does a moving bird represent that which is not? The answer may be sought in the definition of the horizontal line, i.e. heaven and the viewer's perspective. If a viewer observes the heavens then the bird is underneath a surface of the sky giving rise to the notion of absence, i.e. that which is not there (yet). Indeed, the pictogram for "below" or "lower" is 下 (prn xia) which has a notable similarity. Therefore, it may be inferred here that for the Chinese people the existence of something is defined through the negation of its phenomenal appearance. It is as if what one sees is just a veil that hides underneath the true nature of things and their potentiality to become.

Such a parasight is extremely important not only for its ability to allow one to detect multiple meanings within the same word/symbol, but, most importantly, for its contextual value as a source of multiple interpretations within the same phrase. Instead of mapping one meaning to one symbol, many subliminal meanings can be derived through the position of the letters within a word, a word within a sentence, and the letters within the sentence. In addition, the geometrical forms that compose letters and, by extension, words can also serve as a source of multiple "visual readings".

"Letter" is a notion that differs from that of a "symbol". While, in English, a letter implies attachment to an established alphabetical system, a symbol does not. A letter implies a conventional system in order to derive meaning whereas a symbol can be newly encountered or created and can be added to a list. It is common belief that all letters were originally symbols that were eventually digested into letters. While a symbol suggests flexibility, adaptability, and subjectivity a letter suggests conventionality, rigidity, and objectivity. What makes letters so rigid is the existence of alphabets or any other established group of letters. Because of the seemingly permanent acceptance or recognition of alphabets, letters have followed a rigid path of guarding, reinforcing, and cementing alphabets.

Traditionally, the word alphabet is derived from its first and second letter, i.e. "A" and "B" and not the first and last letter, i.e. "A" and "Ω" (or in English "A" and "Z"). In other writing systems, an alphabet can be a large collection of characters (e.g. Kanji or Hanji; that is, the set of Chinese characters) or a group of single or double sounds such as in Japanese hiragana and katakana. The dominant mode of discussing linguistic formations in the Western word is that of the Greek alphabet in which letters are assumed to be established as a set of a few symbols that over time were expanded, modified, and solidified into what was called an alphabet. The problem with this assumption is that if it was fixed, then it should be called "alpha-omega" from the first and last letter, i.e. "A" and "Ω". In contrast, the word "alphabet" is derived from the first and second letter, implying that the list of following letters can be expanded, perhaps modified and revised. With these operations, a letter can be seen as a starting point for exploring possibilities and expanding established limits. Instead of assuming the fixed existence of 24 letters, new letters can be added, some letters can be subtracted and others may be replaced. Rather than mapping a fluid and expandable world of knowledge to a fixed set of letters, a more consistent, coherent, and predictable mapping could exist instead. In addition, the formation of words, that is, groups of letters, would be enhanced, expanded, and evolved to form new words from new letters that perhaps will map the knowledge they represent more accurately, coherently, and consistently.

Let's consider the following example. "Word", itself as a term, differs from, but is often confused with, the term "verb". While in English a verb is a word that indicates action, etymologically they are both derived from the same Latin root, the word verbum. In turn, the Latin word verbum is derived from the Greek word ειρω (prn ero), which means say, speak, or tell. However, in Greek the word for "word" is λέξις (prn lexis), which is derived from the root λογος (prn logos), which means narrate, explain, reason. So, in that sense, according to the Greeks, a word is not only a phonetic utterance but, most importantly, a logical element. Instead of basing communication on a temporary composition of vocal sounds as the former definition does, the latter emphasizes its permanent logical composition. Rather than using sounds that could easily be misunderstood, mispronounced, or misused by the speaker or the listener, a written word is defined through a geometrical pattern whose visual value is irrelevant to the writer or the reader. In addition, a written pattern can be decomposed in simpler forms in two dimensions while a vocal word can only be decomposed in one dimension; that is, linearly. In this context, a word can be seen as a logical structure composed of smaller elements (e.g. letters that form a basis upon which synthesis is possible). What makes this assumption so problematic for linguists is that they have maintained an ethics of complexity and arbitrariness in the discipline. Because of their simplicity, letters are seen as arbitrary vocal elements of language, and by definition, irrelevant to the logical structure of the word. Instead, the meaning of a word is derived from its mappings and not its internal logical structure. Interestingly, this is not the case in other languages, namely Chinese, where words are unarguably deriving their meaning from the synthesis of constituent symbols and radicals. Interestingly, the Chinese word for "word" 語 means crime of the mouth (言). However, there is another definition of the word "word" and it is 辭 , which is composed of two parts: 爵 , which means resolve, and 辛 , which means sin. So, word is that which you need or use to resolve an offense, such as seriously offending superiors. It is not a communication device alone but rather a means of expression, explanation, and reasoning.

Instead of accepting the dominant linguistic view that words are arbitrary constructions, an alternative possibility could be explored in which words are assumed to be the result of letter constructions. Rather than looking at each word as an arbitrary mapping for describing a language, a word is decomposed further into archetypical symbols, which will be called letters. These letters, which are meaningful symbols, can then, through as system of logical rules, form words. New words can be formed through application of the rules as well as other words can be excluded due to lack of application of the rules. Previous linguistic theories in this direction have involved mere phonetic, poetic, or emotional interpretations of letters.

In that sense, a letter is seen as a vocal sound that is generic and primitive enough to represent a basic concept. Unlike Chinese, where every symbol represents a noun, what if letters are symbols that represent verbs? For instance, "A" is not denoted as a starting point (i.e. a noun, adjective, adverb, or preposition), but rather the action of starting, i.e. a verb. By doing so, one can limit the amount of basic actions and construct a short set of symbols, something impossible in the Chinese language. There every object in the world has to be represented with a symbol, such as a man (人), a woman (女), a child (子), a tree (木), a mouth (口), big (大), or above (上). Reversely, actions can be limited to any number, based on the observer or the observed. For instance, for a baby its actions can be limited to those of eat, sleep, and pee/poo.

So, by that definition, a baby's alphabet would consist of three letters, which correspond to these three basic actions. As actions in life increase, so do the letters, which correspond to these new actions. So, if there is a way of determining a small set of basic actions then an alphabet could be constructed out of these basic actions. It will then serve as a building block to synthesize words that will encapsulate both the meaning of the letters analytically and the meaning of the word synthetically. Any word can then be understood in, at least, two ways at the same time. Further, the sequence of letters can reveal the rules that construct the word but also the history of the word. For instance, two letters "M" and "N" would create a new word "MN" that has a new meaning on its own but also the two original meanings of the two letters on the background. The sequence "first M then N" will reveal the order, history, and rules of creation. In this case, if MN exists but NM does not exist, then the sequence is very important.

Let's consider a 24 × 24 table for each letter in the Greek alphabet so that all possible pairs (or diphthongs) are created: ΑΑ, ΑΒ, ΑΓ, ΑΔ, ΑΕ, etc. until ΩΩ. Then, each pair is compared against each word in Homer's Odyssey so as to determine how many times it is found. The table is shown as Figure 2.1.

Each pair shows the number of unique appearances (see below each pair); for instance, the pair AB is found in 55 words (e.g. ΛΑΒΗΣΙΝ, ΚΑΒΒΑΛΕ, ΡΑΒΔΩ, ΒΛΑΒΕΤΑΙ), etc. The pairs that are colored dark grey indicate same letter pairs. The pairs colored in light grey indicate uni-directionality (e.g. MN is found in 148 words but the opposite NM is found nowhere). The empty cells indicate that the pair is not found anywhere (e.g. ΒΓ or ΓΒ).

Interestingly, as mentioned earlier, some the pairs have letters that can be found in one direction but not in the opposite. For example, ΣΤ, ΡΜ, ΜΝ, ΜΠ, ΚΤ are found either in the beginning of the word or somewhere inside the word in over 100 words. However, the opposite pairs (i.e. ΤΣ, ΜΡ, ΝΜ, ΠΜ, ΤΚ) are not found anywhere either at the beginning or inside a word. Never. Not even once. Why? One explanation may be given by phonetic linguistics. Proponents of the phonetic interpretation of letters could claim that some pairs are too hard to pronounce. While this may be true, it is hard to prove the claim since no one knows how each letter was pronounced. For instance, today ΣΤ is pronounced "st" and the opposite ΤΣ is pronounced "ch". Neither one seems too hard to pronounce, at least, today.

Challenging these assumptions, let's assume that each letter in a pair represents an action and that the position of a letter within a word signifies a relationship between the two letters. This means that, for some reason, Σ can be before T, but T cannot be before Σ. The reason could be temporal, cause–effect, visual, topological, location, or simply common sense. For example, it could be that in the same way that a parent can give birth to a child but not a child to a parent, Σ is always before T. But what is Σ and what is T?

Let's assume that every letter of the alphabet represents a verb; that is, an action. Then, there must be twenty-four actions or, for the original version of the alphabet, sixteen. Those original letters are the following:

Α, Β, Γ, Δ, Ε, Ι, Κ, Λ, Μ, Ν, Ο, Π, Ρ, Σ, Τ, Υ.

A	B	Γ	Δ	E	Z	H	Θ	I	K	Λ	M	N	Ξ	O	Π	P	Σ	T	Y	Φ	X	Ψ	Ω
AA 58	BA 200	ΓA 243	ΔA 322	EA 278	ZA 18	HA 51	ΘA 503	IA 425	KA 719	ΛA 578	MA 566	NA 742	ΞA 187	OA 19	ΠA 603	PA 570	ΣA 1011	TA 1220	YA 67	ΦA 256	XA 206	ΨA 81	ΩA 10
AB 55	**BB** 2			EB 100		HB 20		IB 106	**KB** 8	ΛB 11	**MB** 59			OB 33		PB 18	**ΣB** 9		YB 43				ΩB 7
AΓ 393		**ΓΓ** 163		EΓ 91		HΓ 91		IΓ 171	KΓ 4	ΛΓ 19				OΓ 40		PΓ 104	**ΣΓ** 17		YΓ 124				ΩΓ 28
AΔ 136	**BΔ** 12	**ΓΔ** 10	**ΔΔ** 1	EΔ 203		HΔ 71		IΔ 432	**KΔ** 4	**ΛΔ** 11		NΔ 110		OΔ 150		PΔ 30	**ΣΔ** 14		YΔ 113				ΩΔ 21
AE 140	BE 76	ΓE 355	ΔE 493	**EE** 213	ZE 143	HE 85	ΘE 648	IE 343	KE 652	ΛE 869	ME 1590	NE 821	ΞE 231	OE 109	ΠE 1012	PE 675	ΣE 1274	TE 160	YE 160	ΦE 208	XE 319	ΨE 63	ΩE 27
AZ 114				EZ 45				**IZ** 141						OZ 3			**ΣZ** 1		YZ 11				ΩZ 1
AH 30	BH 96	ΓH 91	ΔH 203	EH 87	**ZH** 27	**HH** 265	ΘH	IH 421	KH 167	ΛH 409	MH 368	NH 576	ΞH 30	OH 48	ΠH 183	PH 448	ΣH 485	TH 34	YH 21	ΦH	XH	ΨH	ΩH 14
AΘ 205				EΘ 213		HΘ 107		IΘ 185	**KΘ** 2	ΛΘ 62		NΘ 94		OΘ 88		PΘ 43	**ΣΘ** 426	**TΘ** 11	YΘ 128	**ΦΘ** 92	**XΘ** 70		ΩΘ 29
AI 2037	BI 43	ΓI 53	ΔI 268	EI 2080		HI 104	ΘI 116	**II** 24	KI 160	ΛI 438	MI 245	NI 249	ΞI 25	OI 1585	ΠI 363	PI 560	ΣI 1181	TI 457	**YI** 71	ΦI 244	XI 54	ΨI 19	ΩI 28
AK 353		ΓK 41		EK 378		HK 118		IK 347	**KK** 4	ΛK 81				OK 87		PK 40	**ΣK** 229		YK 182				ΩK 64
AΛ 827	BΛ 35	ΓΛ 46		EΛ 771		HΛ 219	ΘΛ 30	IΛ 232	KΛ 205	**ΛΛ** 253				OΛ 437	ΠΛ 192			TΛ 34	YΛ 185	ΦΛ 4	XΛ 18		ΩΛ 49
AM 630		**ΓM** 30	**ΔM** 36	EM 445		HM 265	**ΘM** 38	IM 373	**KM** 15	**ΛM** 43	**MM** 36			OM 725		**PM** 109	**ΣM** 63	**TM** 27	YM 245		**XM** 8		ΩM 148
AN 1210		**ΓN** 71	ΔN 27	EN 2036		HN 734	ΘN 32	IN 1356	**KN** 31	**ΛN** 2	**MN** 148	**NN** 25		ON 2104	**ΠN** 57	**PN** 57		TN 4	YN 378	**ΦN** 18	**XN** 40		ΩN 856
AΞ 52		**ΓΞ** 6		EΞ 217		HΞ 36		IΞ 70		**ΛΞ** 4				OΞ 30		**PΞ** 21			YΞ 73				ΩΞ 6
AO 106	BO 167	ΓO 213	ΔO 357	EO 431	ZO 103	HO 56	ΘO 221	IO 858	KO 495	ΛO 582	MO 437	NO 1109	ΞO 46	**OO** 63	ΠO 808	PO 1047	ΣO 275	TO 1431	YO 121	ΦO 159	XO 263	ΨO 25	ΩO 31
AΠ 441				EΠ 615		HΠ 51		IΠ 259	**KΠ** 20	ΛΠ 31	**MΠ** 107			OΠ 245	**ΠΠ** 42	PΠ 77	ΣΠ 120		YΠ 266				ΩΠ 67
AP 676	BP 79	ΓP 65	ΔP 103	EP 1082		HP 245	ΘP 88	IP 319	KP 215					OP 455	ΠP 261	**PP** 52	ΣP 1	TP 390	YP 320	ΦP 137	XP 83		ΩP 102
AΣ 1285				EΣ 1410		HΣ 1237		IΣ 1250		**ΛΣ** 11		**NΣ** 5		OΣ 1413		PΣ 67	**ΣΣ** 579		YΣ 960				ΩΣ 311
AT 777				ET 796		HT 296		IT 296	**KT** 231	ΛT 9		NT 968		OT 305	**ΠT** 184	PT 105	**ΣT** 639	**TT** 4	YT 226				ΩT 124
AY 229	BY 7	ΓY 93	ΔY 140	EY 718	ZY 15	HY 20	ΘY 122		KY 156	ΛY 315	MY 84	NY 188	ΞY 25	OY 1022	ΠY 97	PY 317	ΣY 122	TY 150		ΦY 148	XY 33	ΨY 13	ΩY 1
AΦ 139				EΦ 245		HΦ 27		IΦ 95	**KΦ** 11	ΛΦ 10	**MΦ** 140			OΦ 119		PΦ 27	**ΣΦ** 60		YΦ 68				ΩΦ 10
AX 147		**ΓX** 50		EX 159		HX 40		IX 127	**KX** 2	ΛX 2				OX 99		PX 76	**ΣX** 133		YX 107				ΩX 15
AΨ 20				EΨ 37		HΨ 1		IΨ 39			**MΨ** 32			OΨ 18		**PΨ** 7			YΨ 58				ΩΨ 1
AΩ 95	BΩ 34	ΓΩ 48	ΔΩ 112	EΩ 188	ZΩ 75	HΩ 23	ΘΩ 78	IΩ 156	KΩ 92	ΛΩ 192	MΩ 109	NΩ 274	ΞΩ 25	OΩ 109	ΠΩ 96	PΩ 284	ΣΩ 104	TΩ 205	YΩ 41	ΦΩ 50	XΩ 57	ΨΩ 15	**ΩΩ** 12

2.1 A 24 × 24 table for each letter in the Greek alphabet showing all possible pairs of letters

The number of letters could increase over time as more actions are added, but at some point there were just sixteen.[4] Each letter must have a meaning associated with it so that they can function as the building blocks of a language. By combining letters, one can combine actions to produce more complex actions, beyond the original sixteen. Let's also assume that two actions make a noun, or, in other words, two verbs make a noun. This is the opposite of Chinese. In Chinese, two or more nouns can make a verb.[5]

While nouns are time-independent, verbs are not. Verbs denote actions and, as such, are based on time: past, present, and future, or combinations thereof. So, when referring to a verb there must be a way to distinguish time. That would be denoted either by the grammar or by the syntax of letters. So, for example, if vowels were to denote time then their use or position within a word would denote when the action occurred. Suppose that the letter A denotes the "potential to become" (therefore something between present and future), E denotes past that was completed (past tense), or O denotes an "endless repetition". So, in that context, for the letter B there would be three possibilities: "BA", "BE", and "BO". If, for example, B means "to live", then BA would mean "to live in the future", BE would mean "to live in the past", and BO would mean "to live forever".

Letters are symbols and, as such, have a visual appearance (see Figure 2.2). Their shape is important in identifying them. Regardless of their pronunciation, which admittedly can alter over time, shapes are timelessly unaltered. A circle, for example, will always be a circle regardless of how it is pronounced.[6] Furthermore, geometrical shapes have visual qualities that allow one to express, understand, and interpret certain meanings. A line, for example, has a beginning and an end whereas a circle has no beginning or end. A triangle has three points. A wedge shows direction.

The letter Γ (gamma) resembles a wedge. A (alpha) looks like a wedge with a line in the middle. K (kappa) is a wedge with a line at the tip of the wedge. Δ (delta) is a wedge with a line at the open end of the wedge. Σ (sigma) is two Γ (gammas) and B (beta) is two Δ (deltas). E is three wedges whereas Y is a wedge with a line at its tip. Λ, M, and N look like one, two, and two interlocked wedges respectively. Sometimes the wedges are placed horizontally (A, B, Γ, Δ, E, K, P, Σ) and sometimes they are placed vertically (Λ, M, N, Y). Wedge seems to be an important symbol component.

What is the meaning of a wedge? Perhaps, action; maybe the action of becoming. Rather than indicating the existence of something, the wedge denotes its potentiality. It symbolizes the beginning, initialization, birth, emergence, and origination. It represents its coming into existence. However, the action of coming-to-be or becoming does not necessarily have to be associated with creation, beginning, or emergence, but rather may denote a process of

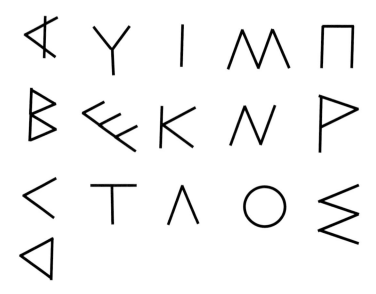

2.2 Greek letters

derivation, transformation, or transition from one state into another. Transition is indeed an act of becoming except its connotation is problematic because whatever is subject to a transformation must already be complete in all its parts, a notion antithetical to the traditional view of creation as an accumulative process. Such an action involves the existential operation of instant becoming. The pre-Socratic philosophers rejected such notion as absurd, because nothing can just come into being or suddenly cease to exist. As they rejected traditional explanations for the phenomena they saw around them in favor of more rational explanations, they also set the limits of human imagination. According to Parmenides, if something came into being, it is not (γάρ εγέντ', ουκ έστιν), i.e. something that pops out of nothing cannot really exist. In the next few paragraphs we will consider a few parasights starting with the word "nothing".[7]

Nothing

In Greek the word for everything is ΟΥ (from Α-ΠΟ > Α-ΠΥ > ΑΥ (Α>Ο) > ΟΥ) which means back, again, anew; that which is not likable, right, or useful. It is an absolute and objective negation of existence, as opposed to ΜΗ, which denotes denial from a subjective point of view.[8]

Nothing is a word that differs from but is often confused with the word empty. Empty is about absence of material substance, either at a phenomenal or physical level, whereas nothing is about the lack of logical existence. The lack of appearance does not necessarily imply the lack of existence. Existence and physical appearance are not identical. Within Greek philosophy nothing is something that is not possible. It is a lie, an illusion, or an error. It does not really exist, has no reality and therefore must be designated as nothing. Similarly, for the Hebrews this same notion has no *hay ah*; that is to say, it is of no effect, no validity and therefore no reality. Nothing is the state out of which God creates the world (i.e. *ex nihilo*) so only He can understand its meaning. So, any attempt by humans to understand its nature is useless, unfaithful, and, as such, hubris.

In Buddhism, however, negativity and non-being are positive and good because the Buddhists take their point of departure in the negative side of life and the world. For them the being of existence is a nothing; likewise non-being is the negation of something negative and is, therefore, something positive. Likewise, in Taoism, nothing is defined as the opposite of something. So, in order for one to understand the meaning of something one needs first to understand the meaning of nothing. The duality of these two antithetical notions, as they co-define one another, gives rise, in turn, to a sense of unity, balance, and harmony. In Lao Tsu's own words, "What *is* is beneficial, while what *is not* also proves useful".[9] Everything is nothing, and nothing is everything.

In early Greek thought there is a strong debate over the nature of nothingness. The significance of its value is argued to lie in its negation rather than in its affirmation. At least two major schools of thought were developed around this idea. The first one, represented by Heraclitus of Ephesus (about 535–475 BC), which, similarly to Eastern philosophy, tries to identify nothing through its opposite, therefore creating an antithetical duality. Nothing is seen as a necessary notion only because it allows the affirmation of something through its own negation. The second school of thought, referred to as the Eleatic, despises the notion of nothing mainly because it doesn't make any sense since it negates rational reality. How could something be if it is not? However, in their effort to prove the preposterous nature of nothingness those early Greek philosophers constructed the following argument: that nothing comes out of nothing and nothing disappears into nothing. In other words, things cannot just pop out of nowhere or suddenly cease to exist. The true nature of things is composed out of an eternal and indestructible substance and as such cannot be nothing. What we observe as empty, absent, or hidden is not an instance of nothing but rather simply a transformation from one state into another in its physical appearance. This argument, while generally attributed to Parmenides of Elea (5th century BC), does indeed seem to have its roots within Eastern philosophies about nothing. The dominance of the Greek philosophy with its written sources and eponymous thinkers has indeed overshadowed Eastern philosophies of the same or former historical periods yet seem to share some common characteristics.

The notion of existence is often defined as the opposite of non-being; that is, that which is not nothing. In English, the word *existence* is derived from the prefix *ex-* (i.e. forth) and the verb *sistere*, which in Latin means to cause to stand up or come to a stop (in turn, derived from the Greek word ἵσταμαι = stand up). Thus, etymologically the meaning of the word existence can be associated with the action of appearance or arising. In Greek, the word existence is ὕπαρξη which is derived from the prefix υπο- (hypo-) (i.e. under, below, or beneath) and the noun αρχή (arche) (i.e. beginning, start, or origin).[10] Thus, existence is not only about the distant past, the beginning of things but also even further, as it involves a step beyond, below, or beneath the starting point. But how is that possible? How can something lie beyond the beginning? Wouldn't that result in a new beginning, which should then be displaced again *ad infinitum*? Such a train of thought may appear paradoxical because it is interpreted as a sequential linkage in the context of a beginning and an ending point. As established earlier, in the pre-Socratic spirit, the notion of a beginning must be rejected (as well as that of an end). Things exist before their phenomenal starting point and therefore the use of the prefix hypo- declares the framework, structure, or platform out of which starting points can be observed. Similar to a river, its origin is not the spring itself but rather lies far beyond, beneath, or below its phenomenal emergence. The true beginning of the river lies not in the spring but rather deep inside the mountain.

Interestingly, as mentioned earlier, in Chinese the character for nothing (or, to be precise, the negation of existence) is 不 (prn bu) which is etymologically linked in the dictionary as a bird rising to heaven. But what does that have to do with nothingness? Why does a moving bird represent that which is not? The answer may be sought in the definition of the horizontal line, i.e. heaven and the viewer's perspective. If a viewer is above heaven then the bird is underneath a surface giving rise to the notion of absence, i.e. that which is not there (yet). Indeed, the pictogram for below or lower is 下 (prn xia) which has a notable similarity. Therefore, it may be inferred here that, similar to the Greeks, for the Chinese the existence of something is defined through the negation of its phenomenal appearance. It is as if what one sees is just a veil that hides underneath the true nature of things and their potentiality to become.

Design is also associated with existence in the sense of creating new things. Similarly, design is usually associated with the derivation of new things that suggests the presence or existence of a new fact, condition, or quality. The word *design* is derived from the prefix *de-* and the Latin verb *signare*, which means to mark, mark out, or sign. In Greek, the word design is σχέδιο (prn schedio), which is derived from the root σχεδόν (prn schedon), which means *nearly, almost, about, or approximately*. Thus, by its Greek definition, design is about incompleteness, indefiniteness, or imperfection, yet it is also about likelihood, expectation, or anticipation. In its largest sense, design signifies not only the vague, intangible, or ambiguous, but also the strive to capture the elusive.[11]

Traveling further back into the origin of the Greek word σχεδόν (prn schedon) one may find that it is derived from the word έσχειν (prn eschein),[12] which is the past tense of the word έχω (prn echo), which in English means to have, hold, or possess. Translating the etymological context into English, it can be said that design is about something we once had, but have no longer. The past tense in the Greek language is referred to as indefinite (αόριστος) and, as such, it is about an event that did occur at an unspecified time in the past, hence it could have happened anytime between a fraction of a second and years ago. So, according to the Greeks, design is linked indirectly to a loss of possession and a search into an oblivious state of memory. This linguistic connection reveals an antithetical attitude toward design, one that, in the Western culture at least, is about stepping into the future, a search for new entities, processes, and forms, frequently expressed by the terms *novelty* or *innovation*.

It appears therefore that the notion of design, according to the Greeks, is associated with the past instead of the future. Such an assumption appears almost antithetical to the predominant notion of design as a process that leads toward the derivation of novelty. How can the past be of such significant importance, especially as a recollection of past lost thoughts? If, according to the Greeks, design is about something that we had but do not have any more, hence it is lost somewhere in the past, what is its connection to something that is about to become into the future, i.e. a novelty? Why would they bring up such an unexpected and obscure relationship? Is it possible that novelty in the sense that we understand it today, according to the Greeks does not exist per se and anything new is just *an illusion*?

If we look deeper into pre-Socratic philosophers such as Xenophanes, Parmenides, or Zeno, one of the common agreements between them was the assumption that nothing comes out of nothing and nothing disappears into nothing; nothing can just pop up or vanish without a trace. Such an assumption is very important to understand their reluctance to conceive, accept, or understand the concept of novelty in its modern sense. If everything is indestructible then change is nothing but a transformation from one state into another; the appearance or disappearance of parts is only phenomenal; nothing is added or subtracted. Therefore, if something emerges, appears, or claims to be new, then it must be nothing but an illusion, because if it is not, then it would contradict the initial premise of preservation. Such logic, while it may appear to be simplistic or absolute, is also very powerful because it does not allow thoughts to be affected by sensory phenomena. What is most significant about this logic is that it sets a paradigm in which knowledge about reality is based upon reason and therefore strives to be truthful, while human opinion of appearance is based upon our senses, which are not only unreliable but also misleading.[13] According to this logic, design as a mental process of creation can be seen as bounded by the limits of preservation: any newly conceived thought, process, or form is nothing but a reordering of previous ones. However, if we consider this possibility, then we are confronted with the problem of origin: as every "new" idea depends on its previous one, then there must be an origin, a starting point, a root or roots out of which everything spurs, tangles, and multiplies offering glimpses of what appears occasionally to be "new". Hence, we are led to the conclusion that the origin, like its material counterpart, must be fixed, eternal, and indestructible. And since novelty involves the negation of existence (i.e. something that did not exist before), novelty is impossible. It is only a sensory illusion.[14]

Novelty therefore must be the result of discovery. While knowledge about the lack of existence is impossible, the lack of knowledge about existence is possible. In other words, the discovery of the existence of something is indeed new, as it pertains to the body of knowledge that it adds to. It is about the existence of something that was, until it was discovered, out of the set of human knowledge. Unlike mere compositional rearrangement of existing elements into seemingly new entities, a discovery is a revelation of something that existed before but was not known.

The same point is eloquently argued by Chuang Tzu: as the origin lies beyond its observable starting point and as the conclusion extends further than its phenomenal end, a need arises to define a world that exists beyond its perceived or conceived reality. "When I look for their origin [that is, of death and life], it goes back into infinity; when I look for their end, it proceeds without termination. Infinite, unceasing, there is no room for words about the Tao."[15] Whether deterministic or accidental such a world is apprehended only through a systematic process of searching and discovering principles that are external, universal, and foreign to human existence. Ironically, those principles can be deduced only through their own absence; that is, the affirmation of their value is done through the negation of their absence. In that case, existence is defined not as the condition that will bring upon something to emerge out of nothing but rather as the condition under which something may not cease to exist. In contrast, nothing is defined not as the existence of the non-existing but rather as the non-existence of the non-existing.[16] In other words, something is not the negation of nothing because then that would mean that something would have to come out of nothing. Instead, something is that which cannot *not* exist and if it appears in different forms it is only because it is changing between different states of existence. This is exactly the same argument that the pre-Socratic philosophers argued: that nothing comes out of nothing and, consequently, everything comes out of something else.

Everything
The English word "everything" or "total" (tous in French, tutto in Italian, and todo in Spanish) is defined as "the whole number or amount of something" and is derived from the Latin word totus, whose origin is uncertain. In Greek, the word for everything is ΟΛΟ (prn olo), which is derived from the past tense of the verb ΕΛΑΩ (prn elao), which means: "to start", which in turn is derived from the verb ΙΑΛΛΩ (prn ialo), which means: "to say". According to this parasight, everything is that which was said. In other words, the notion of a whole is related to language, in the sense of reaching an end to that which can be defined. Incidentally, the word

ΟΛΟ (prn olo) denotes an intellectual whole, as opposed to ΠΑΝ (prn pan), which denotes a material whole. The root of the word ΟΛΟ is ΕΛ.

Possible

The English word "possible" (possible in French, possible in Italian, and possible in Spanish) is derived from the Latin word "potis", which means: "strong" or "able". So, according to this derivation something is possible when it makes itself able to exist. In Greek however, the word for "possible" is ΠΙΘΑΝΟ (prn pithano), which is derived from the past tense of the word ΠΕΙΘΩ (prn peitho), which means: "to convince". So something is possible when it was convinced to exist. According to this parasight, possible is subjective and it is based on a dialogue as opposed to the Latin definition which is based solely on the object's potential to exist. The root of the word ΠΙΘΑΝΟ is ΠΑ.

Random

The English word "random" refers to "something made, done, happening, or chosen without method or conscious decision". It is derived from the French verb "randon", which means: "to run fast" or "to gallop". Similarly, the word "chance" refers to the possibility of something happening. It is derived from the Latin verb "cadere", which means: "to fall". In Greek, the word for chance is ΤΥΧΗ (prn tehe), which is derived from the verb ΤΕΥΧΩ (prn tefho), which means: "to make". According to this parasight, random, chance or luck is not possible to occur without a conscious method or decision. By using the verb "make", in its etymological definition, the maker is connected to the process of making. If we assume that nothing in nature is random and that for every artefact there is a human responsible for its creation, then for everything there is a reason for existence, which results from a related action and, so, humans are responsible for their actions. In other words, chance is not external but rather internal to the subject. The root of the word ΤΥΧΗ is ΤΑ.

Error

The English word "error" (erreur in French, errore in Italian, error in Spanish and irre in German) refers to "the state or condition of being wrong in conduct or judgment". It implies a deviation from a right way, which may, in turn, be defined as the true or correct way. But what is true or correct? The word itself is also derived from the Latin word "erro", which in derived from the Greek word ΕΡΡΩ (prn erro), which means "to walk slowly" or "to hobble". In contrast, the Greek word for error is ΛΑΘΟΣ (prn lathos), which is derived from the present perfect of the verb ΛΑΝΘΑΝΩ, which means: "to forget". So, according to this parasight, to make an error is to have forgotten something. The root of the word ΛΑΘΟΣ is ΛΑΣ.

Truth

The word truth in Greek is ΑΛΗΘΕΙΑ (prn alitheia), which is composed of Α + ΛΗΘΗ, which means not + forgotten. So, according to this parasight, truth is that which you do not forget. The root of the word ΑΛΗΘΕΙΑ is ΛΑΣ.

Art

In English the word "art" (arte in French, arte in Italian, and arte in Spanish) refers to the "expression or application of human skill and imagination". It is borrowed from the Greek word ΑΡΤΙΟΣ, which means: "perfect". However, in Greek the word for art is TEXNH (prn tehne), which is derived from the verb TEYXΩ (prn tefho), which means: "to make", which is derived from the past tense of the verb TIKTΩ (prn tekto), which means "to give birth". Further, the word TIKTΩ is derived from the verb TΛΑΩ, which means: "to suffer, endure, or dare" (i.e. Atlas, the god who carried the sky on his shoulder). So, art according to the Greeks is not the pursuit of perfection, but rather, the struggle and suffering to create something (i.e. to give birth). So, according to this parasight, the pursue or appreciation of art is not in the object of art itself, which may or may not be perfect according to the opinion of the viewers, but rather in the action of the maker who suffers, endures and dares in order to create something new. Incidentally, the word architecture is composed of two parts: archi + tecture. The first part archi is derived from the Greek word APXH (prn archi), which means: "to start" and the second part is derived from the verb TIKTΩ (prn tekto), which means "to give birth". The word APXH, in turn, is derived from the two parts AΡΩ + AΓΩ (pr. aro + ago) which means: "to collect" + "to lead". So, architecture can be defined as "to collect and lead in order to give birth" The root of the word TEXNH is TA.

Sport

The word "sport" in English refers to "the competitive yet entertaining physical activity". This word is derived from the verb disport, which means, "to enjoy oneself unrestrainedly". In Greek, the word for sport is AΘΛΟΣ (prn athlos), which, as the word art, is derived from the same verb TΛΑΩ, which means to suffer, endure, or dare. According to this parasight, sports are not related to personal entertainment or satisfaction but rather to suffering, endurance, and dare. The root of the word AΘΛΟΣ is TA.

Life

The English word "life" is derived from the German word Leif, which means "body". In Greek the word life is BIOΣ (prn bios), which is derived from the future tense of the verb BAINΩ (prn vehno), which means: "to walk, step, go, move, or proceed". Similar words with the same etymology are biograph, base, or basil (i.e. king). The second letter of the alphabet is BHTA (prn beta) and is also derived from the future tense of the verb BAINΩ. The root of the word BIOΣ is BA.

Teach

The word "teach" is derived from the Latin word dicere, which is derived in turn from the Greek word ΔΕΙΚΝΥΜΙ (prn dicneme), which mean: "to show" or "to reveal". The Greek word is ΔΙΔΑΣΚΩ, which is derived from the verb ΔΑΩ (prn dao), i.e. teach, which in turn is derived from the verb TΥΠTΩ (prn tipto), which means: "to tap, hit, or swat". Similar English words with the same etymology as ΔΑΩ are didactic, daemon, Daedalus. The root of the word ΔΙΔΑΣΚΩ is ΔΑ.

Idea

The word "idea" in Greek is ΙΔΕΑ (prn idea) is derived from the infinitive ΙΔΕΙΝ of the verb ΕΙΔΩ (prn ido), which means: "to see". The verb ΕΙΔΩ, in turn, is composed of two parts: ΕΙ + ΔΩ (prn e + do), which mean: "on" + "to hit" (from ΕΠΙ + ΔΑΩ). English words with the same derivation are video, idiot, iso-, and idol. So, according to this parasight, an idea is something that one sees and, as such, is superficial, referring only to the light that hits the eyes and has nothing profound about it. The root of the word IDEA is ΔΑ.

Value

The word "value" (valoir in French, valere in Italian, and valuar in Spanish) refers to "the importance, worth, or usefulness of something" and is derived from the Latin word valere, which is the present active infinitive of the verb valeo, which means "to be able", or "to rule". In Greek the word for value is ΑΞΙΑ (prn axia), which is derived from the verb ΑΞΩ (prn axo) future tense of the verb ΑΓΩ (prn ago), which means: "to lead". The words agony, action, or angel, are products of the verb ΑΞΩ. So, according to this parasight, value is defined as the action of leading others to follow as opposed to the ability to acquire. The root of the word ΑΞΙΑ is ΑΓ.

School

The English word "school" (ecole in French, scuola in Italian, escolar in Spanish and Schule in German) is defined as "an institution for education". In Greek, the word for school is ΣΧΟΛΗ (prn schole), which is derived from the verb ΣΧΟΛΙΑΖΩ, which means: "to relax". It is derived from the word ΕΣΧΟΝ, which is the past tense of the verb ΕΧΩ (prn eho), which means: "to have". According to this parasight, a school is a place to search for that which you do not have. Incidentally, the English words "scheme" and "sketch", also produced from the past tense of the verb ΕΧΩ (prn eho). The root of the word ΣΧΟΛΗ is ΣΑ.

Responsible

The word "responsible" is derived from the Latin word "spondeo", which is derived in turn from the Greek word ΣΠΕΝΔΩ (prn spendo), which means: "to offer in return". The Greek word for "responsible" is ΕΥΘΥΝΗ, which is the product of two words: ΕΥ + ΙΘΥΣ (prn eu + ethis), which mean: "good" + "be" (i.e. "be" in the imperative form). In brief, responsible is "to be obliged to be good". According to this parasight, responsibility lays entirely on the subject and his or her actions to be good. The word ΕΥ is in turn derived from the participle of the verb ΕΙΜΙ (prn eme), which is ΟΥΣΑ (prn usa). In other words, ΕΥ literally means: "she who has become". So, in that sense, good is to be yourself, i.e. complete. The root of the word ΕΥΘΥΝΗ is Ι.

Theory

The word "theory" in Greek is ΘΕΩΡΙΑ (prn theoria), which is composed of two parts: ΘΕΑ + ΟΡΕΩ (prn thea + oreo), which mean "wonder" + "envision" (from ΘΑΟΜΑΙ + ΟΡΑΩ). English words with the same derivation are video, idiot, iso-, and idol. So, according to this parasight, a theory is the result of observation, understanding, and prediction and as such is very profound. The root of the word ΘΑΟΜΑΙ is ΔΑ and the root of the word ΟΡΑΩ is ΕΡ.

Statue

The word "statue" (statue in French, statua in Italian, estatua in Spanish and Statue in German) refers to "a carved or cast figure of a person or animal" and is derived from the Latin word "statua", which in turn is derived from the Greek word ΙΣΤΗΜΙ (prn isteme), which mean: "to stand". In Greek the word for statue is ΑΓΑΛΜΑ (prn agalma), which is derived from the verb ΑΓΑΛΛΩ (prn agallo), which means: "to honor". ΑΓΑΛΛΩ is composed of Α + ΓΑΝΥΜΑΙ, which means: "emphatically" + "to please". Further, ΓΑΝΥΜΑΙ is derived from the verb ΧΑΙΡΩ, which is composed of ΧΑ + ΕΙΡΩ, which means: "joy" + "to say". ΕΙΡΩ is derived from the root ΛΑ (prn la). So, according to this parasight, a statue is something that makes one say joyful honors. The root of the word ΑΓΑΛΜΑ is ΧΑ.

State

The English word "state" (etat in French, stato in Italian, estado in Spanish and Staat in German) refers to "the particular condition that someone or something is in at a specific time" and is derived from the Latin word "status", which in turn is derived from the Greek word ΙΣΤΗΜΙ (prn isteme), which mean: "to stand". English words with ΙΣΤΗΜΙ as the origin are state, status, stand, estate, or overstate. In Greek, the verb ΙΣΤΗΜΙ is derived from the verb ΣΑΟΩ (prn saoo), which means: "to save" or "to protect". Similar words with the same etymology in English are: save, salvage, soma, or Socrates. The root of the word ΙΣΤΗΜΙ is ΣΑ.

Victory

The English word "victory" (victoire in French, vittoria in Italian, and victoria in Spanish) refers to "an act of defeating an enemy or opponent in a battle, game, or other competition" and is derived from the Latin verb "vinco", which mean: "to fight" or "to overcome". In Greek the word for victory is ΝΙΚΗ (prn nike), which is composed of ΝΗ + ΕΙΚΩ, which means "no" + "retreat". Further, ΕΙΚΩ is composed of Ε + ΙΚΩ, which means: "no" + "arrive". So, according to this parasight, to win is deny to somebody not to arrive. The root of the word ΝΙΚΗ is Ι.

Defeat

The English word "defeat" refers to "winning a victory over (someone) in a battle or other contest" and is derived from the Latin word desfacio, which mean: "to unmake". In Greek the word for defeat is ΗΤΤΑ (prn hetta), which is derived from the word ΗΚΑ, which means "smaller", or "less". Further, ΗΚΑ is composed of Η + ΑΚΟΗ, (prn e + acoe) which means: "no" + "sound". So, according to this parasight, to be defeated is to be silent. The root of the word ΗΤΤΑ is ΚΑ.

Name

The English word "name" refers to "a word or set of words by which a person, animal, place, or thing is known, addressed, or referred to" and is derived from the Greek word ΟΝΟΜΑ, which is derived, in turn, from the verb ΝΕΜΩ (prn nemo), which means: "to distribute" or "to allocate". Similar English words with the same etymology as the word "name" are noetic, autonomous, nemesis, nomad, and paranoia. So, according to this parasight, a name is the result of a distribution. In other words, to have a name is to be part of something greater than you. The root of the word ΟΝΟΜΑ is ΝΕ. Incidentally, the name of the mother of ΑΧΙΛΛΕΑΣ (prn Achilleas) is ΘΕΤΙΣ (prn Thetis) who was known as "the name giver" as her name is derived from the verb ΘΕΤΩ (prn theto), which in derived from the future tense of the verb ΤΙΘΗΜΙ (prn titheme), which means: "to put". The verb ΤΙΘΗΜΙ is, in turn, derived from the verb ΤΑΣΣΩ (prn, tasso), which means "to put in order", which is derived from the verb ΤΕΥΧΩ (prn tefho), which means: "to make". The root of the word ΘΕΤΩ is ΤΑ.

Definition

The word "definition" (definition in French, definizione in Italian, definición in Spanish and Definition in German) refers to "a statement of the exact meaning of a word" and is derived from the Latin word "definio", which means: "set a limit, bound, end". In Greek, the word for "definition" is ΟΡΙΣΜΟΣ, which is derived from the verb ΟΡΑΩ (prn orao), which means: "to distinguish". Similar words with the same etymology in English are: horizon, hour, oracle, eureka, and aphorism. Further, ΟΡΑΩ is derived from the verb ΑΕΙΡΩ (prn aeero), which means: "to elevate", which, in turn, is composed of Α(ΠΟ) + ΕΙΡΩ, (prn a(po) + ero) which means: "from" + "to say". So, according to this parasight, a definition is not something to end with but rather a reference point for comparisons and speculations. The root of the word ΟΡΙΣΜΟΣ is ΕΡ.

Beauty

The word "beauty" (beau in French, bellezza in Italian, belleza in Spanish and Belle in German) refers to "a combination of qualities, such as shape, color, or form, that pleases the aesthetic senses, especially the sight" and is derived from the Latin word "bonus", which is a paraphrase of the word "duonus" (i.e. good, brave). In turn, the word duonus is derived from the Greek word ΔΥΝΑΤΟΣ (prn denatos), which means strong or powerful. In Greek, the word for "beauty" is ΩΡΑΙΟ, which is derived from the verb ΟΡΑΩ (prn orao), which means: "to distinguish". Similar words with the same etymology in English are: horizon, hour, oracle, eureka, and aphorism. Further, ΟΡΑΩ is derived from the verb ΑΕΙΡΩ (prn aeero), which means: "to elevate", which in turn is composed of Α(ΠΟ) + ΕΙΡΩ, (prn a(po) + ero) which means: "from" + "to say". So, according to this parasight, beauty is related to distinguishing something over time, i.e. comes on time or with time and has nothing to do with power. The root of the word ΩΡΑΙΟ is ΕΡ.

Design

The English word "design" (design in Italian, diseño in Spanish and Design in German) is defined as "the art or action of conceiving of and producing such a plan or drawing" and is derived from the Latin word "designo", which is composed of the words "de" + "signo", which means: "from" + "to mark" (i.e. derive a mark). In Greek, the word for design is ΣΧΕΔΙΟ (prn schedio), which is derived from the verb ΣΧΕΔΙΑΖΩ, which means: "to relax". It is derived from the word ΕΣΧΟΝ, which is the past tense of the verb ΕΧΩ (prn eho), which means: "to have". Similar words with the same etymology in English are scheme and sketch. According to this parasight, design is the action of searching for that which you do not have now but had before. In an intellectual sense, searching for a thought that you once had is called "recalling the oblivious". The root of the word ΣΧΕΔΙΟ is ΣΑ.

Notion

The English word "notion" (notion in French, nozione in Italian, and nocifin in Spanish) is defined as "a conception of or belief about something" and is derived from the Latin word "notus", which is derived from the Latin verb "nosco", which means: "to know". The verb nosco in turn is derived from the Greek verb ΓΙΓΝΩΣΚΩ (prn gignosco) which means: "to discern". In Greek, the word for "notion" is ΕΝΝΟΙΑ (prn ennia), which is derived from the verb ΝΕΜΩ (prn nemo), which means: "to distribute". According to this parasight, a notion is the result of a distribution. In other words, to conceive a notion is to discern something greater than its obvious appearance. The root of the word ΕΝΝΟΙΑ is ΝΕ.

Learn

The English word "learn" (apprendre in French, imparare in Italian, aprender in Spanish and lernen in German) is defined as "gain or acquire knowledge of or skill in (something) by study, experience, or being taught" and is derived from German verb "lernen", which means: "to learn". Similarly, the word "apprehend" is derived from the Latin word apprehendere, which is composed of ad + pre + hendere, which mean "toward" + "before" + "to hold". In Greek, the word for learn is ΜΑΝΘΑΝΩ (prn manthano), which is composed of two verbs: ΜΑΩ + ΤΙΘΗΜΙ which mean: "to desire" + "to put". According to this parasight, to learn is to have a desire to put things together, i.e. to order. Note that there is no reference to any benefit to the learner (i.e. acquisition) but rather a natural inclination towards creating order. The root of the word ΜΑΝΘΑΝΩ is ΜΑ.

Genius

The word "genius" (genie in French, genio in Italian, genio in Spanish and Genie in German) refers to "exceptional intellectual or creative power or other natural ability" and is derived from the Latin word "genus", which means "birth" or "origin". In turn, the word genus is derived from the Greek word ΓΕΝΟΣ (prn genos), which means "birth" or "origin". In Greek, the word for "genius" is ΕΥΦΥΗΣ, which is composed of two parts: ΕΥ + ΦΥΩ which mean: "good" + "to bring to light". Similar words with the same etymology in English are: phenomenon, phase, fantasy, photo, or epiphany. So, according to this parasight, a genius is not one who creates through extraordinary powers but rather one that brings the light of knowledge. The difference is that if knowledge is like light, then a genius is simply a medium though which lights is reflected, not necessarily the creator of light. It is a matter of discovery versus invention. This difference is important, as it reveals a fundamental difference between the origin of knowledge being not within the human mind but rather through it. The root of the word ΕΥΦΥΗΣ is ΦΑ.

New

The English word "new" (nouveau in French, neovo in Italian, nuevo in Spanish and neu in German) is defined as "not existing before; made, introduced, or discovered recently or now for the first time" and is derived, according to Wiktionary, from the Proto-Indo-European néwos, which means "new"[17]. In Greek, the word for new is NEO (prn neo), which is derived from the word ΝΗΠΙΟ (prn nepio), which means "infant" and is composed of two parts: ΝΑΩ + ΒΙΟ (prn nao + bio), which mean: "to overflow" + "life". The verb ΝΑΩ is a shortcut from the verb ΝΑΣΣΩ (prn nasso), which is composed of two parts: ΕΝ + ΑΣΣΟΝ (prn en + asson), which means: "was" + "closer". Further, ΑΣΣΟΝ is the comparative adjective to ΑΓΧΙ, which means: "close", and which is derived from two verbs: ΑΓΩ + ΑΧΟΣ (prn ago + ahos) which mean: "to lead" + "anxiety". According to this parasight, new is not something that did not exist before but rather something that always existed except with variable distance from the observer (which in turn produces anxiety). In other words, depending on the distance from the object more or less of its identity is revealed to the subject-observer. Novelty is not a matter of sudden emergence out of nowhere but rather the result of shifting through a revelatory distance towards something that always existed but we did not see. The root of the word NEO is ΑΓ.

Index

The English word "index" (index in French, indice in Italian, índice in Spanish and Index in German) is defined as "an alphabetical list of names, subjects, etc., with references to the places where they occur, typically found at the end of a book" and is derived from the Latin word "indicō", which means "to point out, show". In turn, the word "indicō" is derived from the Greek word ΕΝΔΕΙΚΤΗΣ (prn endiktis), which is composed of two parts: ΕΝ + ΔΕΙΝΚΥΩ which mean: "were" + "to show". In Greek, the word for "index" is ΕΥΡΕΤΗΡΙΟ, which is derived from the verb ΕΥΡΙΣΚΩ (prn euresko), which means: "to find". This, in turn, is derived from the verb ΕΟΡΑΚΑ (prn eoraka), which is the present perfect of the verb ΟΡΑΩ (prn orao), which means: "to observe". Further, ΟΡΑΩ is derived from the verb ΑΕΙΡΩ (prn aeero), which means: "to elevate", which in turn is composed of Α(ΠΟ) + ΕΙΡΩ, (prn a(po) + ero) which means: "from" + "to say". Similar words with the same etymology with ΕΙΡΩ in English are: irony, rhetoric, or martyr. According to this parasight, an index is not only a means to reference words but also a means to understand something. The root of the word ΕΥΡΕΤΗΡΙΟ is ΕΡ.

Notes

1. One possible derivation of the verb "to see" is from the Greek σάω = θεάωμαι, ὁρῶ.

2. The word *statuere* is derived from the Greek word ἵστ-ημι (prn ist-eme) which means to stand up. The root ιστ- (prn ist-) is still embedded into words such as assistance, circumstance, distance, insistence, existence, resistance, etc.

3. Similarly, the word beauty in Greek is ὡραῖο (prn oreo) and is rooted in the word ὥρα (prn ora), which means time. So, beauty according to the Greeks comes at the right time or in time. However, in English the word beauty is derived from the Latin word bonus, which is a paraphrase of the word duonus (i.e. good, brave). In turn, the word duonus is derived from the Greek word δυνατός (prn dunatos), which means strong, powerful.

4. Before Palamidis added Θ, Φ, Χ, and Ζ and Simonidis (4th century) added Η, Ξ, Ψ, and Ω.

5. For example, the verb "run" (走) is composed of a person leaning forward (夭) and a foot (止).

6. This is true also in Chinese characters. They have a geometrical appearance that has not altered over time while the pronunciations of the Chinese people change over time and location. While Mandarin and Cantonese are quite different languages when heard, the symbols they use are the same. A newspaper can be read in all parts of China.

7. Along the line of pre-Socratic thought, the prefixes a-, un- or in-, when used in the sense of negation, opposition, or contrast to reality, are absurd, confusing, and pointless. Either something exists or not. The preposterousness that is inherent in the negation of existence is very apparent in two linguistic constructions, namely the words *unknown* and *unreal*. Both are terms that while they exist as words yet they are both preposterous.

8. See Βασδέκης Ν. Σ., Ἐτυμολογικό Λεξικό τῆς Ἑλληνικῆς Γλῶσσας (www.paramyths.com/lexikon).

9. See verse 11 in Tzu Lao, *Tao Te Ching*, Hamill, S. (trans.), Boston: Shambahala Publications, 2005.

10. Alternative versions of the word ὕπαρξη (i.e. existence) in Greek are ὑπόσταση, which is equivalent to *ex-sistere*, and τό ὄντι, which literally means *this which is*. Ὄν (prn on), which is the root of the word ontology, is the present participle of the verb εἰμί (i.e. I am).

11. Precisely, the root of σχεδόν (prn schedon) is derived from ἔσχειν (prn eschein), which is the past tense of the verb ἔχω (prn eho), that is, *to have*. Therefore, design is literally about the reminiscence of a past possession at an indefinite state and at an uncertain time. Similarly, the word scheme, from the Greek σχῆμα, means shape and is also derived from the root σχεδόν.

12. ἔσχειν (prn eschein) is also the root of the English word *scheme*.

13. The Socratic analogy to shadows in a cave illustrates the illusion-prone nature of the senses and the inability to distinguish reality (light) from its representation (shadow). The feeling of sensory illusion is so comfortable that attempts to reveal their deceptive nature is met with fierce resistance (Republic, book VII). While in Plato's dialogue *Parmenides* there is a clear distinction between the Socratic theory of ideas and Parmenides' existential philosophy, both are in agreement on the deceptive nature of the senses.

14. To paraphrase a paradox by Zeno, a student of Parmenides, it can be argued that novelty resembles an arrow moving forward in time and as a moving arrow either it is where it is or it is where it is not yet. If it is where it is, then it must be standing still, and if it is where it is not, then it cannot be there; thus, it cannot change position. Of course, the paradox is just a symbolism of the inability to achieve something out of nothing, i.e. to create something new.

15. See Tzu Chuang, 25.11.

16. Ibid., 22.8.

17. It is clear to anybody who studies the facts of history, that the Greeks produced an amazing culture that spans all possible dimensions of the human mind: from philosophy to medicine and from technology to art. The only means to produce such diverse knowledge is a common platform upon which these accomplishments can be derived. That platform is, and must be, language, because that is the only thing that is different from so many other cultures that, albeit similar, did not produce the same quality, quantity, and diversity of work. So, to circumvent their language using an obscure other culture, the so-called Indo-European, who left no comparable culture whatsoever is, apart from ludicrous, also highly suspicious. It reminds one of the story of a child who claims that the cookies eaten from the jar were not the child's actions but rather those of a thief who entered in the house only to steal those cookies. Of course, it is possible, but extremely unlikely. Even if it was slightly possible that such an Indo-European culture did exist that fed the Greeks with their language, why is that important? It is as if for the work of a great chef we praise the farmer instead.

– 3 –

Digital Culture: A Critical View

THIS chapter may appear contradictory at times, not because of the quality of information or the complexity thereof but rather because of a shift in linguistic meaning in the technological jargon today. Over the last few decades, words have changed meaning in such a way that the same word means something completely different from what it meant a few years ago, resulting in confusion, misunderstanding, and contradiction. For instance, consider the title of this chapter: *digital culture*. Even the phrase "digital culture" is a contradiction. On the one hand, culture can be defined as something entirely human that involves arts, literature, religion, or philosophy. It is the subjective realization, understanding, and expression of a group of humans at a particular time in history. It is about our thoughts, dreams, aspirations, and fears. On the other hand, digital is something objective, quantifiable, neutral, and therefore non-subjective. It is about precision, finite, and countable. So, from the very beginning we're called upon to define the relationship between two antithetical terms: digital and culture. It is almost the same as trying to define what "subjective objectivity" is about.

Let's start with a myth, an ancient Greek myth which may illustrate metaphorically this contradiction. It is the myths of Theseus' ship or rather the paradox of Theseus' ship. Theseus was a hero in the ancient Greek mythology who had done many great deeds, such as defending the people of Athens from monsters, daemons, and thieves, going to the island of Crete and killing the Minotaur, saving people from disasters and famine, founding cities, and many more. Theseus did his heroic deeds by using his ship which he loved dearly. It was that ship that took him to foreign lands, let him escape from dangers, and opened new sailing paths for him. When he got old, he anchored his ship at the port of Athens. But the ship was made out of wood and over time it started to deteriorate. First, the sail fell off. So, Theseus ordered it to be replaced. Then the mast collapsed, only to be replaced immediately. Then the rows, the ropes, the flags, and then the hull fell apart. He ordered all of them to be replaced with new ones. Eventually, at some point the entire ship was replaced with new parts and even though it looked the same, none of the original parts was present. And so, a question arises: which one is Theseus' ship? The ship that he sees in front of him today or that ship that remains in his memory? Is that deck that he is walking on today the same deck as the one that he jumped on when he was fleeing from the Cretans years ago? Does the sail he sees today on the ship be the same sail that years ago caused his father's death? Is that mast the same one he climbed to see his beloved Ariadne when he fell in love with her? Does it matter which one is the real one? Is not what we see, touch, smell, hear, and taste the same thing as that which is in our minds? If we still use the same words to identify something, shouldn't they mean the same thing? Or is there something deeper, something behind the visual appearances that contains a meaning that cannot be defined with words?

Design in the last few years has gone through a similar transformation. Words that were used as recently as twenty years ago today mean something entirely different, if not antithetical. Technical terms that are used in design to convey a concept, a technique, or a process have changed in such a way that their meaning is completely different, leading to confusion, misunderstanding, misconceptions, and contradictions. Let us consider the process of design as a sequence of actions: starting with an inspiration, followed by a sketch, a blueprint, a model which is then rendered and finally presented to convey the original thought. So, we can say with a certain degree of certainty that even today the process of design has a starting point into the world of ideas and is progressively materialized into a more specific form that is then sent for implementation. Let us define these stages using the following words: inspiration, modeling, rendering, and presentation. So, within this paradigm, design starts with an idea, a concept, and an inspiration that initiates the process. Then the designer needs to make the idea more specific by using a pencil and paper to sketch out the main form. Then more details are added in order to produce a working model. Next, the designer is in a position to render the model in the order to convey the material and formal qualities. However, in the world of design today the process of modeling has been enhanced and to a certain degree replaced by computer programs such as autoCAD, Rhino, or Maya. Let me explain what I mean by the term "replace": by using computer programs the designer gets results that are often unintentional, unpredictable, and unexplainable and when that happens a black box is set between intention and action. What used to be done manually using paper and pencil has been distanced by using a mouse and a virtual screen. Moreover, the process of producing a model has been enhanced, corrected, altered, and modified often with no direct control by the user of the software. This causes a great problem in the design process because for the first time the user becomes unaware of the behavior of the tools. While such discrepancies of tools may have been encountered before such as spills, breaks, or scratches of brushes, now the result is mostly intellectual. Computer tools produce results that, when viewed by the designer, appear to be intelligent. Yet, while some of that intelligence may be credited to the developers of the software, there are increasingly more cases where even the developers are also unaware of the intelligence of the results of their own software. The lack of human control in the process of intelligent behavior is problematic. I will try to demonstrate this problem in the remainder of this chapter. Let's start with some obvious and easy-to-understand examples. Rendering used to be a manual, tedious process involving artistic skills, perspective geometry, painting, and, occasionally, collage, not to mention being time consuming and expensive. Today, computer programs such as V Ray, Renderzone, or Maxwell provide virtual reality representations that often exceed the real not only in the accuracy of depiction but also in their ability to extend reality into artificial, illusory, and fantastic worlds. Meanwhile, the speed, efficiency, and cost of such rendering mechanisms are far distanced from their original manual process. Further, the techniques, processes, and methods of presentation of models have also altered so much from the world of manual presentation so that the terms used today serve no help in demoting what really is happening and are therefore confusing and misguiding. For example, there is little if nothing photographic about Photoshop and the word Illustrator offers no connection to the profession of an illustrator at least as it is remembered some twenty years ago. Similarly, Rhino, Grasshopper, Maya, or max are part of a nomenclature that provides very little to address, define, and explain the logic, structure, and potential of digital systems.

Consider the image shown in Figure 3.1. The object on the left side is the result of a device called a laser cutter. This device uses a laser beam to make precise incisions on paper or balsa-wood. Twenty years ago, if a student presented me with such a model I would have immediately praised that person. It would have meant that this student would have possessed amazing abilities of precision, patience, dexterity, agility and perhaps innovativeness in order to accomplish it at such a level of perfection. Today, if a student comes to me with such a model I would not be impressed at all. In fact, some professors who are not aware of this potentially deceptive situation praise the students to which they gladly accept the praise. Similarly, the object on the right is a 3D print and not a traditional sculpture. Twenty years ago this would be a true exhibition of talent, adeptness, elegance, and self-discipline. Not any more. The distance between the artist's hands and the object of his or her artifact has been permanently and irreversibly distanced if not severed. Let me be more specific. Consider a painting such as the one shown in Figure 3.2. Is it really a painting? Or simply the application of Photoshop filters upon a digitized photograph? Eighty years ago such a painting may have altered the history of art, initiating a period of art referred to as impressionism, not to mention the price of such a piece of art, perhaps, invaluable. Today it is just one of the many filters of Photoshop, this one perhaps appropriately named "impressionistic". The list goes on and on. From makeup photographs that depict an impossible reality to renderings of imaginary places that become indistinguishable from real places. The reverse is also true. Consider the picture shown in Figure 3.3.

Is this a computer graphics image or a real city? Is it a series of copy and paste that goes on and on until the end of the virtual landscape or actual houses where people live? The answer is that this is a real city. It exists in the real world. Actually, it is a housing development of about 10,000 low-income houses in Ixtapaluca, a suburb of Mexico City. The question here is whether reality itself has been affected by virtual reality instead of the other way around. In other words, did the digital process of copy and paste have an effect in the design of the housing project and consequently in our understanding of reality? Or is it that our understanding of reality incorporates digital elements to such a degree that it has become part of our everyday interpretations either conscious or unconscious?

This may sound like the chicken and egg problem. In other words, is it the chicken that made the egg or is it the egg that made the chicken? Or to paraphrase a bit, is it reality that makes the digital or is it the digital that makes reality? Despite its banal trivialization, it is a very

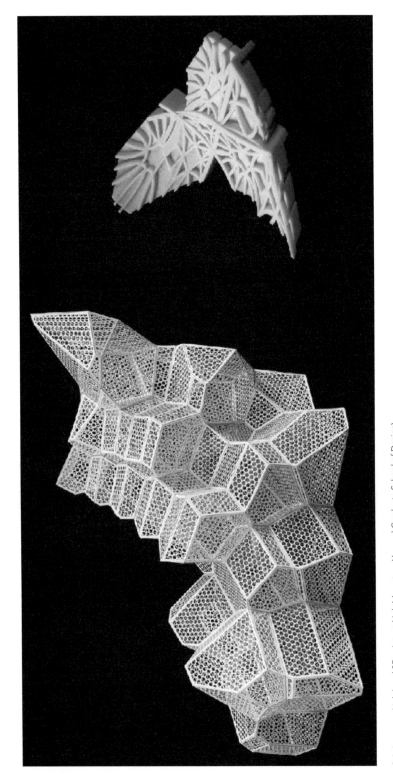

3.1 Laser-cut (right) and 3D printout (right) (courtesy Harvard Graduate School of Design)

3.2 A photograph (top) and the application of an impressionistic filter by Adobe Photoshop on the same photograph (bottom)

3.3 A bird's eye view of the settlement Ixtapaluca in Mexico

important problem because it addresses the mystery of creation and visual appearances. Perhaps there is an answer to this problem that may be offered to us as a possible and interesting solution: perhaps the problem exists in the first place because of a confusion in distinguishing reality from appearance. What if the chicken does not exist? What if the chicken is simply a cover-up, a disguise, a technique that the egg employs to make more eggs? This possibility may not be as crazy as it may seem at first glance if we redefine the concept of reality. In Platonic terms, real is that which does not change. So, if a chicken is changing in the way it appears due to time, character, behavior, quality, deterioration, or other physical idiosyncrasies, then according to Plato it is not real. On the other hand, the idea of an egg as a means for procreation is constant and does not change over time and space. So, perhaps, the egg is the only real thing in the chicken–egg paradox. The same is true for other relationships of a phenotype-genotype nature. Just because we can see, hear, taste, smell, or touch something that does not make it real despite the sensory certainty. What something really is may not be found in its appearance but rather behind it in a much deeper level that one may not be aware of, and yet, that constant notion is its real essence. Simply enjoying a form without questioning it would only be "philosophically irresponsible".

As a consequence, words in the vocabulary of the designer today have changed meaning, especially with the emerging application of computational methods. Most of the terms have been replaced by computational counterparts and we should probably take that as a sign that something is happening in the world of design, something very important, fundamental, and profound that may have strong influences and repercussions. From Photoshop filters to modeling applications and from simulation programs to virtual reality animation and even more mundane tasks that used to need a certain talent to take on, such as rendering, paper cutting, or 3D printing/sculpting, the list of tasks diminishes day by day being replaced by their computational counterparts. What used to be a basis to judge somebody as a talent or a genius is no more applicable. Dexterity, adeptness, memorization, fast calculation, or aptitude are no longer skills to seek for in a designer or reasons to admire in a designer as to be called a genius. The focus has shifted far away from what it used to be toward new territories. In the process many take advantage of the ephemeral awe that the new computational tools bring to design by using them as means to establish a new concept or form only to be revealed later that their power was based on the tool they used and not on their own intellectual ability. After all, the tool was developed by somebody else, the programmer, who, perhaps, should be considered the innovator if not the genius.

As a result of the use and abuse of design tools many have started to worry about the direction that design will take in the next few years. As one by one all design tasks are becoming computational, some regard this as a danger, misfortune, or in appropriation of what design should be and others as a liberation, freedom, and power toward what design should be, i.e. conceptualization. According to the second group, the designer does not need to worry any more about the construction documents, schedules, databases, modeling, rendering, animation, etc. and can now concentrate on what is most important: the concept. But what if that is also replaced? What if one day a new piece of software appears that allows one to input the building program and it produces valid designs, i.e. plan, elevation, sections that work? And, worse, what if they are better than the designer would ever do by himself or herself? Even though most designers would never admit that something is better than what they would have designed on their own, yet what if deep inside them they admit the opposite? What then? Are we still going to continue demonizing the computer and seeking to promote geniuses when they really don't exist? Or should we reconsider our knowledge, terms, concepts, processes, and methodologies and seek for new answers rather than old reassurances?

In this context, as a scholar, I set out to inquire into these matters in a rather serious manner. Increasingly, I became aware of the possibility that something paradigmatic is emerging in the world of design through my computational research as a professor and a practitioner. As a small contribution, I ended up writing numerous experimental software programs, papers, and published three books.

The first book is titled *Expressive Form: A Conceptual Approach to Computational Design* by Spon Press and was published in September 2003 with a foreword by the late Bill Mitchell. It is about the notion of expressiveness in architecture through the use of computational and computer-based methods. In this book I tried to offer computational directions, which combine theoretical questions with practical implementation. The notions of exaggeration, hybridization, kinesis, algorithm, fold, and warp are being investigated in the light of their computational and formal value. Each notion is examined from different points of view; that is, historical,

3.4 *Expressive Form*

mathematical, or philosophical. The aim of the book was to provide a conceptual basis for computer-aided design but to remove the treatment of the subject away from the promotion of certain software packages or modeling approaches, and also away from the more hyperbolic and woolly texts that deal with the impact of digitalization on architecture and contemporary life.

  The second book is titled *Algorithmic Architecture* and was published by Architectural Press/Elsevier in June 2006. It provided an ontological investigation into terms, concepts, and processes involved in algorithmic architecture and set a theoretical framework for design implementations. The structure of the book did not follow a traditional theory-based philosophical book format. It was not a computer programming/language tutorial book either. Even though there were a series of design works illustrated, it was not a design/graphics art book per se. Following the tradition of architecture as a conglomeration of various design fields, namely engineering, theory, art, and recently computation, the challenge of the book was to present a concept that, like architecture, is a unifying theme for many diverse disciplines. An algorithm is not only a computer implementation, lines of code in a program, or a language, but also a theoretical construct with deep philosophical, social, design, and artistic repercussions. Consequently, the book presented many, various, and often seemingly disparate points of view that led to the establishment of one common theme which was the title of the book.

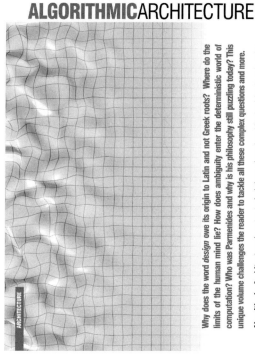

ALGORITHMICARCHITECTURE

TERZIDIS

Why does the word *design* owe its origin to Latin and not Greek roots? Where do the limits of the human mind lie? How does ambiguity enter the deterministic world of computation? Who was Parmenides and why is his philosophy still puzzling today? This unique volume challenges the reader to tackle all these complex questions and more.

Algorithmic Architecture is not a typical theory-based architectural book; it is not a computer programming or language tutorial book either. It contains a series of provocative design projects, and yet it is not just a design or graphic art book per se. Following the tradition of architecture as a conglomeration of various design fields – engineering, theory, art, and recently, computation – the challenge of this book is to present a concept that, like architecture, is a unifying theme for many diverse disciplines. An algorithm is not only a step-by-step problem-solving procedure, a series of lines of computer codes or a mechanistic linguistic expression, but is also an ontological construct with deep philosophical, social, design, and artistic repercussions. Consequently, this book presents many, various and often seemingly disparate, points of view that lead to the establishment of one common theme: algorithmic architecture.

Kostas Terzidis is Associate Professor at the Graduate School of Design, Harvard University, USA

ISBN 0-7506-6725-7

3.5 *Algorithmic Architecture*

3.6 *Algorithms for Visual Design*

The third book is titled *Algorithms for Visual Design* and was published by Wiley in 2009. It offered a series of methods in the form of algorithms that addressed new concepts in digital design in a way that is applicable, generalized, and inspirational. Questions such as: how do I create an ordered composition using random patterns, how do I create a hybrid form that resembles two other forms, why is it that some patterns express self-similarity, or how is it that certain processes even though random behave as self-organizing aggregations? The book offered a series of generic procedures that can function as building blocks for designers to experiment, explore, or channel their thoughts, ideas, and principles into potential solutions. The computer language used is a new, open source, and easy-to-use language called processing used quite extensively in the visual arts in the last few years. The algorithms and techniques are quite advanced and offer not only the means to construct new algorithms but also function as a way of understanding the complexity involved in today's design problems.

Then, a series of events were initiated under the title "Critical Digital". Critical Digital was an idea originally conceived by doctoral students under my supervision when I first arrived at Harvard's University Graduate School of Design in 2004. We started the idea of organizing events as a means to address the various and diverse issues raised from the digitalization of architecture. Our efforts led to a series of symposia held at the GSD in 2005, 2006, and 2007. In 2008, some of the students in the Doctor of Design program took on the idea and developed it into the form of a wiki-conference called "What Matter(s)?" It was a great success! In 2009, this effort led to a second conference called "Who Care(s)?"

It is important to point out here that these were not conferences in the traditional sense of a descriptive event often self-congratulatory, but a dialogue, an inquiry, and a struggle aimed at questioning what is rapidly becoming the de facto mainstream. What is digital? Why should design be (or not be) digital? How have practitioners and schools been using digital media? We were not concerned with the "how" question but rather with the "why" question. Why digital? Why not? Why so? Why us? Why now? Why here?

It was clear to us then, as it is now, that we are and will be dependent on computational technology both in practice as well as in academia. This fact ought to raise critical questions not only about the mundane use of computational technology in studio, competitions, or in the building process itself but also more deep and profound questions of identity, authenticity, or responsibility at least on the side of the designer. The question is who the designer is today and how important are one's own ideas versus the techniques provided in an increasingly digitally dominated world. It may be claimed that the use of computational technologies in design, as well as in everyday activities, has deep and profound consequences not only in the way thoughts and ideas are conceived, understood, and communicated but also in their intrinsic value and validity. Is it possible to design without a computer today? Is it that digital techniques have become determinant conditions, perhaps hidden, upon which the designers, practitioners, or critics base their ideas, thoughts, or even ideologies? How important is it for designers to know the mechanisms of software or hardware and therefore the limits that these technologies impose on design and does that even matter any more?

Second International Conference on Critical Digital

Who Cares(?)

17-19 April 2009

Harvard University Graduate School of Design,
Cambridge MA 02138 USA

Call for papers:
Extended abstracts (500 words) due January 23, 2009

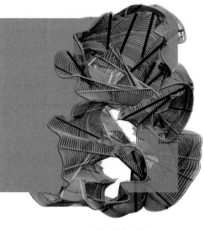

First International Conference on Critical Digital:

What Matter(s)?

18-19 April 2008

Harvard University Graduate School of Design,
Cambridge MA 02138 USA

Call for papers:
Extended abstracts (1000 words) due January 11, 2008

3.7 The proceedings from two conferences held at Harvard University Graduate School of Design

The theme of the first conference was "What Matter(s)?" What matter(s) in terms of work, process, and thought(?) What is the nature of virtuality, ephemerality, continuity, materiality, or ubiquity, which while originally invented to explain digital or computational phenomena, are utilized today in the context of a traditionally still material-based design? Is materiality subject to abstract digital concepts? Is the digital buildable? What matters?

In the same exploratory spirit, the theme of the second conference was "Who Cares(?)" There the question raised was to identify who the designer is today and how important are one's own ideas versus the techniques provided in an increasingly digital dominated world. Is it possible to design without a computer today? Is it that digital techniques have become determinant conditions, perhaps hidden, upon which the designers, practitioners, or critics base their ideas, thoughts, or even ideologies? How important is it for designers to know the mechanisms of software or hardware and therefore the limits that these technologies impose on design and does that even matter any more? Who can take a position about this situation? Who cares enough to question the mainstream?

As an epitome of all this theoretical and critical investigation, I embarked on a series of prototypical design projects where I wrote the computer code in order to explore, experiment, and verify the practicality of these theories. The first series of projects are based on the concept of hybridization (also known as morphing). This was the topic of my Master's thesis back in 1989. Basically, morphing is a visual process in which an object changes its form gradually in order to obtain another form. In other words, morphing is a gradual transition that results in a marked change in the form's appearance, character, condition, or function. The operation of morphing consists basically of the selection of at least two objects and the assignment of a number of in-between transitional steps. The first object then transforms into the second in steps (see Figure 3.8). The essence of such a transformation is not that much in the destination form but rather in the intermediate phases these transformations pass through, as well as in the extrapolations, which go beyond the final form. Morphing is about the transitional continuity of a form that progresses through a series of evolutionary stages (see Figure 3.9).

Another area of experimentation is that of stochastic search. Here, by the term "stochastic search" I mean a random search in space until a given condition or set of conditions is met. Let me give you an example: the placement of toys in a playpen so that each toy does not overlap the others and they all fit within the limits of the playpen can be addressed with a stochastic search. Figure 3.10 shows a stochastic search in 3D space where overlap is permitted and required. Now, stochastic search can also be seen as a method for generating designs of buildings.

3.8 Transition of a square into a triangle. The in-between shape is four-sided topologically but resembles a triangle geometrically

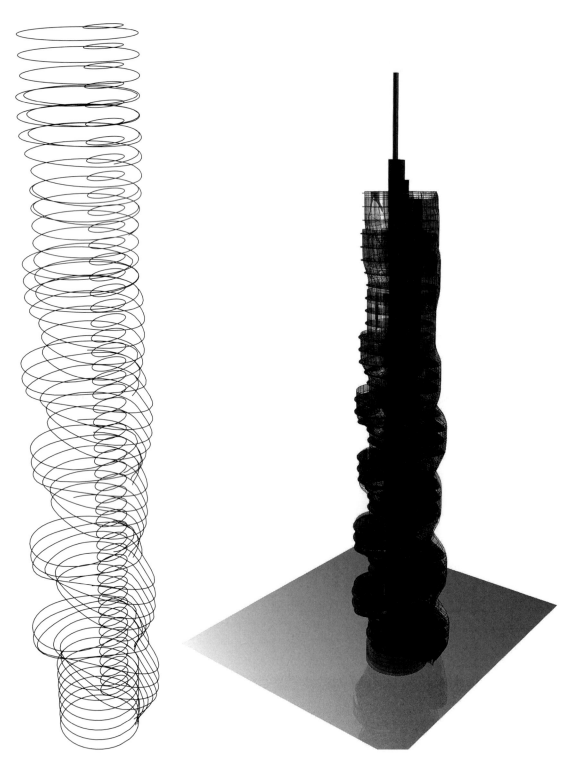

3.9 High-rise studies based on shape transitions

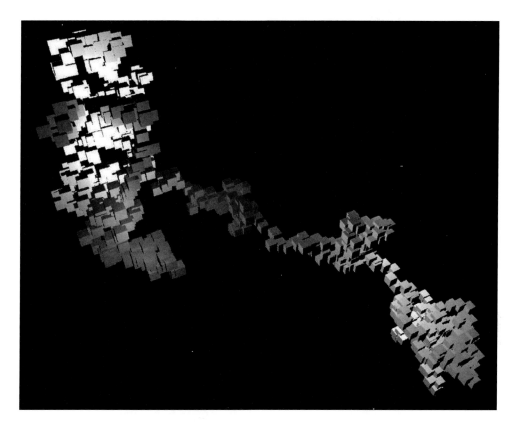

3.10 A series of cubes that demonstrate stochastic search

In Figure 3.11, a series of conditions are set and the building's program grows until the conditions are met. As you may notice, each floor has a different plan, similar to a tree, because every apartment occupant had set different conditions. Compare that with modern-time buildings where each occupant is assumed to be very alike if not identical.

Another algorithm is that of cellular automata. An automaton is a self-acting element and "cellular" refers to the accumulation of many automata into a group. These accumulations are usually arranged along a grid. So one cell like the black one shown in Figure 3.13 can do something that may affect its neighbor shown here in gray. What is interesting about cellular automata is the emergence of unpredictable behavior of the whole when each automaton does something within its own local domain. What I mean by that is that each local behavior contributes to a global behavior that is not always predictable.

Let's take an example: suppose that we start with a grid of randomly assigned black or white cells. Then we set the following rule for every cell: look around you: if you have three black neighbours then you become black otherwise if you have five or more black neighbours then you become white. Now, such a rule while simple on the individual cell's level produces a far more complex behavior if applied repeatedly to the whole. See the result for fifty iterations in Figure 3.14.

3.11 High-rise studies based on stochastic search (class project by Julie Kaufman and Brian Price for course GSD 2311 taught by Kostas Terzidis in Fall 2004 at Harvard University)

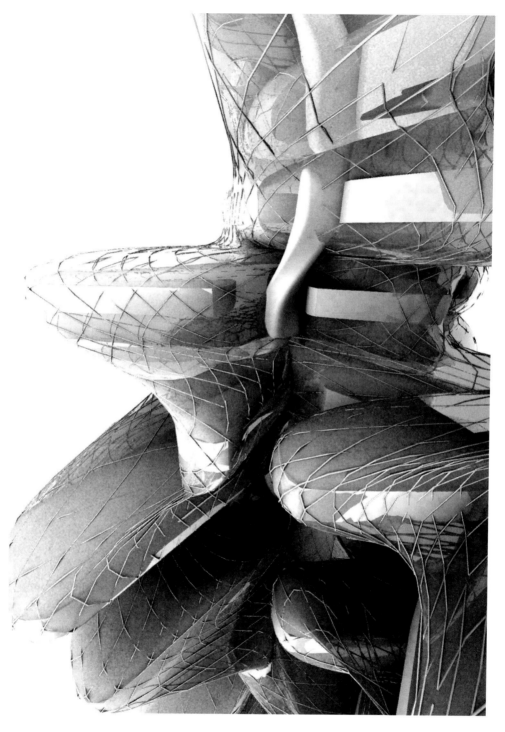

3.11 continued

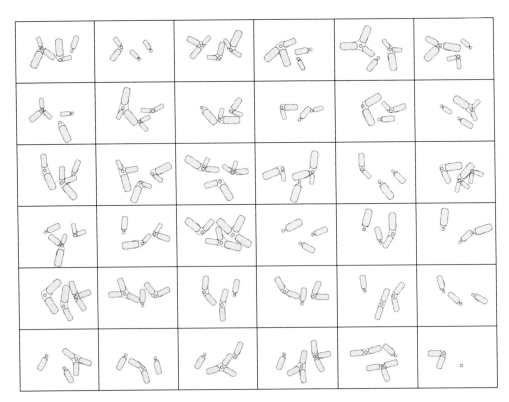

3.12 Interlocking tower plans for each floor of project shown in Figure 3.11

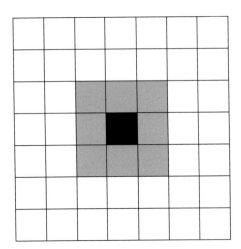

3.13 A cell (black) with its neighboring cells (gray)

The result is a pattern that resembles a maze. It can be used to create a hypothetical mind game of finding a path from A to B. In other words, the local behaviors resulted in a global behavior that appears to have a purposeful existence when obviously it does not. I assume here that purpose is a unique privilege of the living organisms. Now, while this is a simplistic version used for presentation purposes, more complex rules can be devised to reflect design conditions that may result in a more complex building pattern. For example, the number of rooms, their connections, access, view, gravity, energy, price, etc. can be used as rules that will affect the overall pattern of random blocks as shown in Figure 3.15.

Another algorithm that I experimented with was a genetic algorithm. A genetic algorithm

3.14 Cellular automata progression on one to fifty generations and a path to go through the maze is also a stochastic process where guesses are tested as a genetic code using cross-over and mutations repeatedly over large populations. A series of architectural projects were developed on that concept one of which is shown here. Taro Narahara, one of our Doctoral students, developed the underlying algorithm for this project.

Again, all of these projects were interesting yet not fulfilling. All projects were fun, I was using software, I had a theory, I was being appreciated by students, many people liked them, they were published in magazines, but they didn't really satisfy me. Because there was something about this work that I was not happy with. I did not see an egg, only a chicken in this work. It was always superficial, looking nice and skin-deep. I wanted to go beyond the obvious, get deeper into the true nature of computation. So, I developed a theory that I think is an interesting one but nonetheless can be also viewed as an anti-human theory of design, in the sense that it

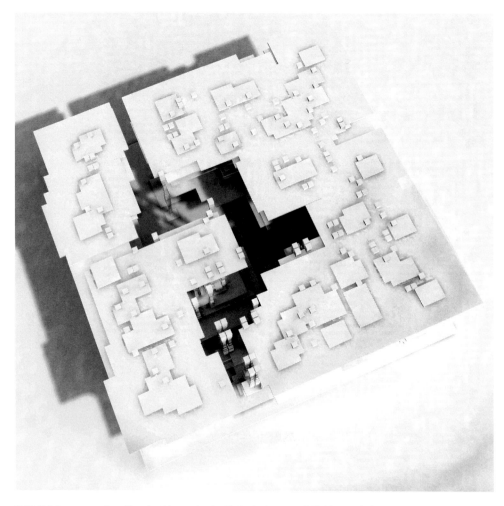

3.15 Cellular automata-based housing (class project by M. Snyder for course GSD 2311 taught by Kostas Terzidis in Fall 2005 at Harvard University)

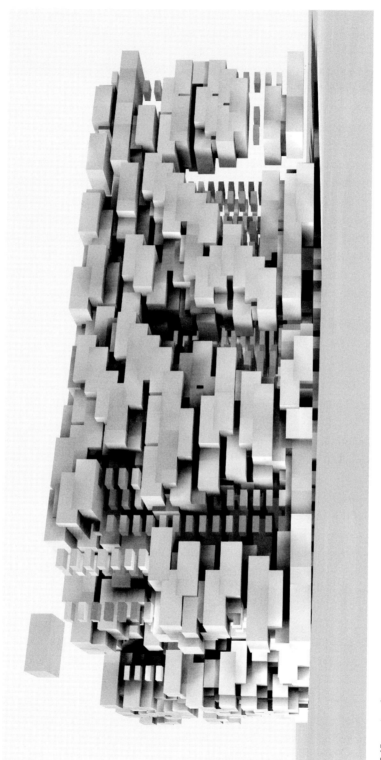

3.15 continued

takes away from you anything that is related to your intentions, ideas, or decisions and replaces it with a completely random set of events; and that randomness strangely enough does not result in chaos but instead in a very interesting order.

It may be that this theory is important only because we are still considering design in terms of an old paradigm that is based on human intelligence and initiative. Is it possible that this paradigm is not valid any more? Is it possible that design is more than just a human activity and as such can be performed by non-humans? Let me illustrate what I mean with a few examples: if a designer wants to draw a dot on a piece of paper, most likely what one would do would be to take a pen or a pencil and lower it on to the canvas marking a dot. But the process involves, apart from mechanical actions, an intellectual determination of the process of lowering the arm and pointing. Strangely enough even though, at first sight, the process appears to be random most of the process is predetermined in the brain as the hands move down. The process can be said to be similar when using a digital tool instead of a pencil. Suppose that you are faced with a canvas in Photoshop and you select a pen and then move the cursor on the screen until you press down on the screen leaving a mark. I see little difference between the digital and the physical process. Now, consider the following commands on a computer system:

```
x = 20
y = 30
point(x, y)
```

This will draw a point at location 20, 30. Replace these commands with the following:

```
x = random(0,100)
y = random(0,100)
point(x, y)
```

I assume that the canvas is 100×100 pixels wide. Also, I assume that a command called random(min, max) exists that can produce an unpredictable (to me) number within a range set between min and max. Now, there is a lack of control/prediction of where a dot will show up. I know that I will see a dot but it is almost impossible to predict its location in advance. Consider also the following commands:

```
x = random(0,100)
y = random(0,100)
if x > 50 and y<50 then point(x, y)
```

Now, I am not only uncertain about the location of a dot on the canvas but I am not even sure if I will see a dot at all. That is, in the case x <= 50 then point() will not be activated. You may start to distinguish a difference between the human world and the computationally driven random world. There is a thin blue line that separates the two. The first is the human world with its intentions, mistakes, aspirations, etc., a world we have been familiar with for over thousands of years. The second world is new, non-human, encountered for the first time; alien and strange. Please cross the line between predictable and unpredictable.

Now let's implement this theory using a simple human task, that of solving a puzzle (see Figure 3.16). Suppose that you are presented with a puzzle composed of ten pieces that

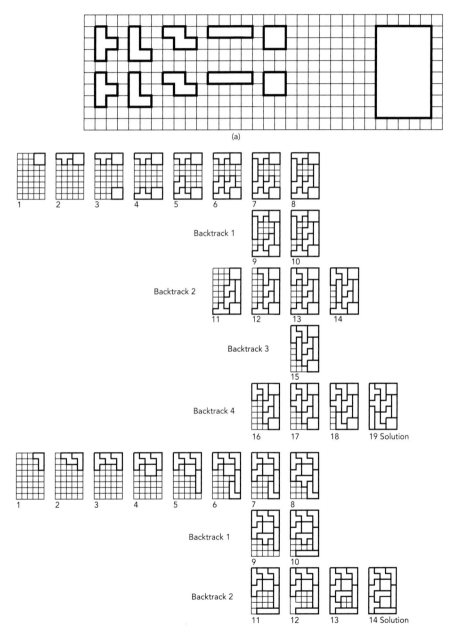

3.16 Intelligent puzzle-solving problem

eventually fits into a rectangular canvas. Any human (consider, for example, a child) will start by selecting the first piece and placing it in the canvas, then the next one and placing it, then the next and so on until either all pieces match or in case there is a impasse, take out a piece or two and rearrange until a match is found. This process may take a few seconds or minutes depending on the complexity of the puzzle or the capabilities of the solver and it is considered as a task of human intelligence, or intelligence in general. Now consider the following possibility. I take the pieces of the puzzle and toss them in the air, let them fall and hope that a match is found. If it does not work I do it again; and again; and again. Over and over; hoping for a match. What are the chances that a match will occur? Most people will say impossible. And yet simple logic may reveal that while a match is unlikely to come soon, yet, logic says that it must occur. Necessarily, by definition the chance must exist since I am referring to it as a possibility. Given enough time there is a possibility, once in a billion perhaps, that it will happen. Actually, we can calculate that number with accuracy and determine the maximum number of attempts that it will take for it to occur. However, nobody will try this method mainly because there is no time to wait. But with a computer such logic starts to be applicable. A billion, for example, is not such a big number. Think of a GHz: this is one billion of cycles per second. So, let's try this process through a computer program. In the first trial, it took 1,252 unsuccessful attempts to get a match, taking virtually only 169 milliseconds. Next time it took 2,619 (or 274 milliseconds) unsuccessful attempts until a perfect match occurred. So, if you were to choose between the two methods you are faced with the following dilemma: should I employ my intelligence and take several minutes to solve the problem or use a mindless chance mechanism and solve the same problem in just a few milliseconds? To some people this is a very fundamental question.

Here is another related problem: how many possible ways can we solve this puzzle? Are there infinite ways or is there a specific number of possible permutations? Let's take a set of nine positions arranged in a 3×3 grid and assume that each position can be either black or white as shown in Figure 3.17. What are the chances that a cross-configuration will occur? In fact, the pattern we are looking for (when laid out) is 010111010, assuming that 1 represents a black box as shown in the patterns below. One way to find out is to start doing random configurations until we get a match. But that may involve repeated patterns and it may take redundantly more time than by using a different method. The second method uses a simple enumeration of permutations starting with a 000000000, then 000000001, then 000000010, and so on. The pattern we are looking for, that is, 010111010, will occur somewhere between 000000000 and 111111111. All possible combinations are 512, or 2^9. The pattern we are looking for comes after 325 attempts (depending on the method or direction of enumeration).

Now in design, although not the same, we have a similar process. In design, and, in particular, architectural design, the problem that a designer is called upon to solve can be regarded as a problem of permutations; that is, the rearrangement of design elements within a set of discrete positions, such as a grid, until a solution is found that satisfies a set of criteria. Traditionally, such arrangements are done by human designers who base their decision making either on intuition (from the point of view of the designer) or on random sampling until a valid or valid solutions are found. However, in both cases the solution found may be an acceptable one but

3.17 All 512 possible permutations of nine boxes arranged in a 3 × 3 grid

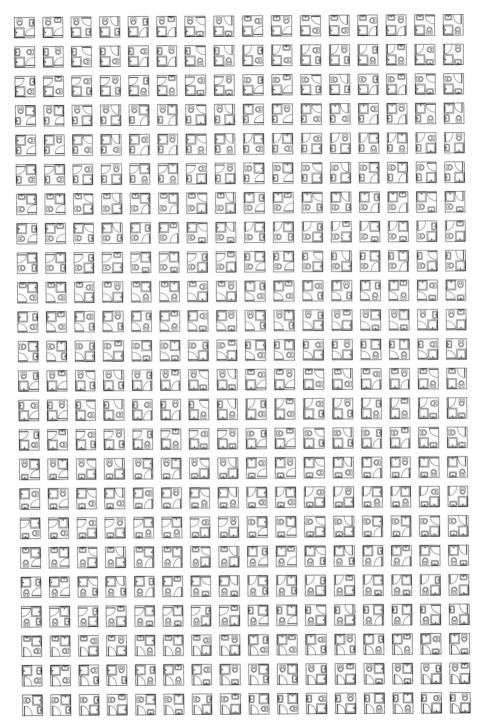

3.18 All the possible arrangements of a simple four-fixture bathroom (this page). These non-repetitive, rotationally specific arrangements are 384. However, after eliminating all arrangements that have a toilet seat facing a door and eliminating any arrangement that uses more than 6m of pipelines (i.e. choosing the least expensive ones) the number of successful bathrooms is only 8 (overleaf)

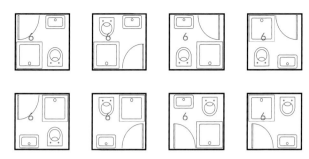

3.18 continued

cannot be labeled as "the best possible solution" due to the subjective or arbitrary nature of the selection process. In contrast, an exhaustive list of permutation-based arrangements will eventually reveal the "best solution" since it will exclude all other possible solutions.

Let's consider the design of a simple bathroom in an architectural plan consisting of four fixtures: a sink, a toilet, a shower, and a door arranged in a 2×2 grid. Figure 3.18(a) illustrates all possible arrangements of such a simple four-fixture bathroom. The number of non-repetitive, rotationally specific arrangements is only 384. However, after eliminating all arrangements that have a toilet seat facing a door and eliminating any arrangement that uses more than 6 meters of pipelines (i.e. choosing the least expensive ones) the number of successful bathrooms is only eight (see Figure 3.18(b)). It can be claimed therefore that these eight bathroom configurations are indeed the best possible ones since they exclude anything else. Of course, we may have to redefine the term "best" and apply it only to quantitative criteria and pertinent only to the number of possible permutations. In other words, given the number of all possible permutations, the resulting eight are the ones that satisfy our constraining criteria and are therefore considered to be the best.

Let's now look at another example. Consider a sample architectural problem, relatively simple for the time and size of this book. I will try to demonstrate the use of permutations as a method for the automatic generation of building plans. In this case, consider a site (b) that is divided into a grid system (a). Let's also consider a list of spaces to be placed within the limits of the site (c) and an adjacency matrix to determine the placement conditions and neighboring relations of these spaces (d). One way of solving this problem is to stochastically place spaces within the grid until all spaces are fit and the constraints are satisfied. Figure 3.19 shows such a problem and a sample solution (f).

So, let's run this algorithm and see the results: after 274 random attempts a solution is found. If we do it again, another solution is obtained and so on. According to this algorithm, each space is associated with a list that contains all other spaces sorted according to their degree of desirable neighborhood. Then each unit of each space is selected from the list and then one-by-one placed randomly in the site until they fit in the site and the neighboring conditions are met. If it fails then the process is repeated. Since the total number of units of all spaces is equal to the site's grid units, there will always be a fit. To illustrate the point, in Figure 3.20(a) nine randomly generated plans are shown as a result of this algorithm. Then each plan is extruded

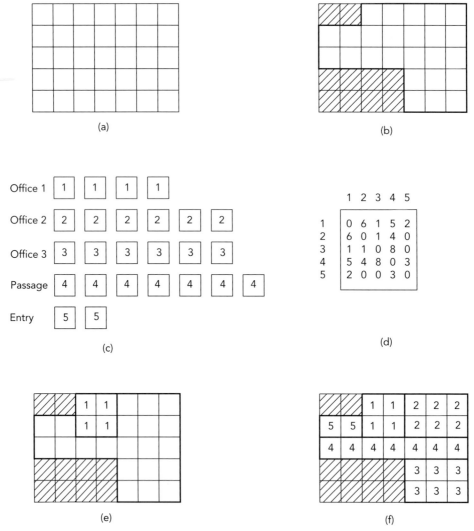

3.19 A site (b) that is divided into a grid system (a), a list of spaces to be placed within the limits of the site (c) and an adjacency matrix to determine the placement conditions and neighboring relations of these spaces (d). The allocation of one space is shown in (e). A sample solution is shown in (f)

into an architectural structure (b) to be potentially stacked into floors. While the algorithm can generate many different solutions, as shown in (d) my research will seek to produce all possible solutions, that is, all possible permutations. If that happens, then we can select from the exhausted permutation list the ones that best fit the programmatic, economic, ecological, aesthetic, or other criteria of the client.

While the previous example is quite simplistic compared to the number of possible arrangements involved in an actual architectural design, nevertheless it illustrates the potential of a system of permutations and presents a different way of approaching architectural design. As I mentioned earlier, the speculation of this work is to detect, test, and implement the use of

3.20 Three stochastically generated plans that fulfill the requirements of the architectural program (a). These plans were then extruded (b) exhaustive permutations as a means of synthesis for architectural plans of buildings. Such an effort involves the risk of increased complexity as the numbers of permutations increase exponentially. While the number of all possible permutations can be pre-estimated using polynomial theory, the actual production of these arrangements may involve algorithms that are np-complete, that is, possible to solve but would require an extremely long time to execute. As an alternative, optimization techniques and, ultimately, brute force techniques can be used instead but, of course, those would depend on the computational power of the computers used.

Another example of architectural permutations was developed by Shohei Matsukawa together with this author. This set involved 3D spatial arrangements of walls, openings, and voids in a two-storey single family house. The series of permutations were evaluated on the basis of orientation, position in the site, program, connectivity matrix, and price of materials. The results are shown in Figure 3.21.

3.21 Alternative buildings (by Shohei Matsukawa)

Another model of using permutations is that of linguistics. Here the results are more impressive mainly because of the power of language to convey concepts using representations that we refer to as words. This is different from visual representations mainly because of the immediate nature of graphics as opposed to the implicit mapping of symbols to concepts as demonstrated in the linguistic world. So, one of the first experiments is to use a set of words and then rearrange them in all possible ways selecting the ones that are syntactically correct. In this case, I selected the following words "If", "it", "exists", "you", "can", "think", "of", "it". These compose the starting phrase shown in Figure 3.22.

Some of the resulting valid permutations are shown in Figure 3.23.

3.22 A human-created sentence

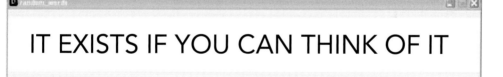

3.23 A series of word rearrangements that are syntactically correct, yet one expresses a profound meaning

While some of the resulting sentences may be expected, some may not. The last sentence "it can think of you if it exists" is grammatically correct, like all the others, yet it conveys a strange meaning. Who is thinking of whom? Obviously, I do not claim that the computer knows the meaning of the sentence and composed it intentionally. Rather the result is profound to us who can interpret it as such. If intentionality is omitted from the process of creation, then the resulting sentence becomes important too. Exhaustive permutations can generate a series of all possible sentences, out of which most make no sense, others make sense but are expected, and perhaps, one or a few make sense and are profound. By thinking alone, one is limited by one's own thoughts and cannot see possibilities that may lead to new ways of thinking. Either because of bias or lack of knowledge certain paths of thinking are not employed. On the other side, computers have no bias or lack of knowledge. They are quantitative machines that methodically and objectively pass through all possible combinations. But they cannot judge the sentences they produce.

An automatic text generator has been constructed that generates stories based on characters and behaviors. One alternative of the narrative generator is this travelers' log where a path is decided and then a story is generated (Figures 3.24, 3.25, and 3.26).

The simulation is based on people's behaviors (birth, marriage, death, conflict, ethical and economical rules).

Haiku, fairy tales, and syntax analysis are methods of approaching language without intentional content. Through permutations poems, stories, or narrations can be constructed that while making sense they are non-intentional. There is no author to claim intentionality. Some refer to the author as the author of the author; that is, the software author is the author of the story. But that is not true. What if software is written that constructs algorithms that produce stories? In that sense, the algorithm becomes the source of intention. This can be illustrated with the following example: suppose that there are three characters each with a set of characteristics taken from the real world (in other words, these characters exist). Now a software developer creates a series of possible combinations that these three characters can be related. Then another software developer writes an algorithm that randomly picks one of the combinations. What if the result is a story whose content none of the characters or authors expected to see? The following story is one such story based in three characters, Pilo, Maki, and Neri. The combinations are many and vast out of which only a few were selected. Here is one story:

Pilo and Maki got involved on June 2, 2005.
She loved him but he was in love with another woman.
Before they got married Pilo had a bad feeling about her relationship.
She asked her friend Neri for advice.
Neri told Pilo to break up.
Pilo did not follow Neri's advice.
Pilo married Maki on September 13, 2005.
Pilo gave birth to little Gigi on March 25, 2006.
She loved Gigi very much.

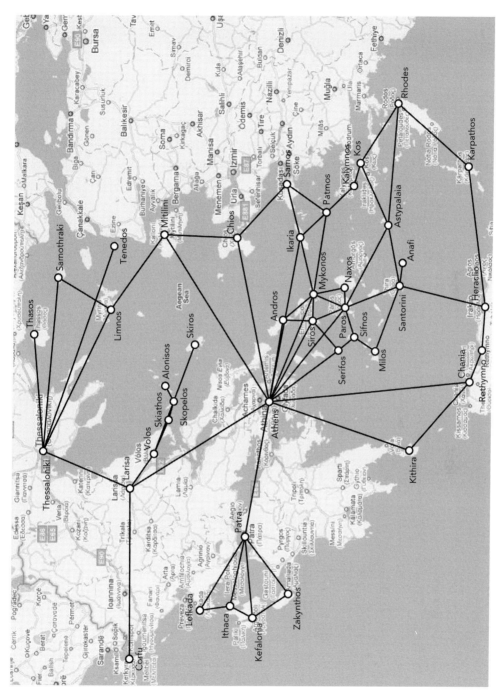

3.24 Map of Greece with major ports

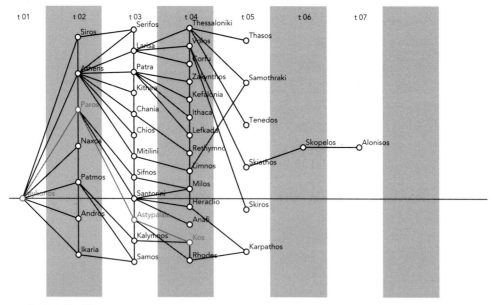

First, I started from Mykonos.
It has 7 connections: to Siros, Athens, Paros, Naxos, Patmos, Andros, and Ikaria.
Consequently, I chose to go to Paros. Paros is a large port.
It has 7 connections: to Athens, Siros, Sifnos, Naxos, Santorini, Astypalaia, and Mykonos.
Consequently, I decided to go to Astypalaia.
Astypalaia is a small port.
It has 4 connections: to Paros, Kos, Santorini, and Rhodes.
So, I decided to go to Kos.
And that is it.

3.25 Map of Greek major ports' path sequence. A story of the decision-making process is articulated in words

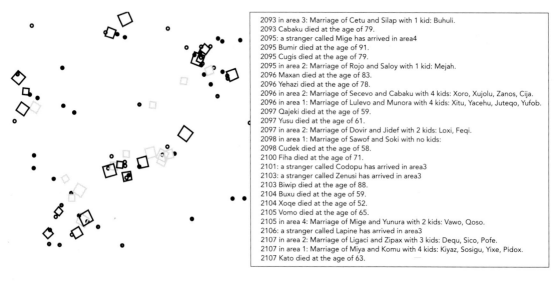

3.26 Agent-based simulation of genealogical patterns and resulting settlement construction

Maki and Neri got involved on May 3, 2006.
Maki divorced Pilo.
Maki loved Neri very much.
. . .

The story is interesting for many reasons but the most important is that there is no author. The behavior of the characters was not predictable by the author (that is, me). Personally, I, as the author, do not accept, approve, or endorse Neri's and Maki's behavior. If I were to intentionally rewrite the story it would be completely different. However, as a reader, I am pretty impressed with the story and would like to read more. What happened next? What is Pilo's reaction? If I am not the author of the story, then who is? Who am I? Does it matter, since I am not in control? Or am I?

I would like to conclude this chapter now with a few arguments based on the book so far. The computer is not a tool only. It is much more than that. It is an intellectual entity and as such can simulate human thinking producing inferior, similar, or even superior results to those of a human mind. Some people do not like that comparison and perhaps there is a merit in that assessment. So, perhaps a better way to describe the computer is that of complementary, alien, or different. Perhaps it has a different way of thinking, a new way, a strange way. I would like to believe that it is complementary in the sense that it can address many of the things we cannot, or better, do not have enough time to deal with.

This brings up the next point: that of the human mind. I am afraid that it is limited. Whether we like it, believe it, or accept it, it is true. Factually true. If you do not believe me try dividing 22 by 7. Or try to plot all the connections on a social network. Or think of architectural complexity in a skyscraper. We are not as smart as we think or want to be. Yet, honestly, I do not want to be too smart, I do not want to learn everything, or do everything. But I would like to know that one day I can break out of that limited world and do something more. Not alone but with help. Well, that is what the computer is: a ticket to that world. It is not a device that replicates what you already know. That would be redundant and useless. That would simply be like re-inventing the wheel. Unfortunately, that is what some designers do. Many think that computers are screens that replace light rays with pixels. I would like to suggest doing things that you cannot do or think in this world with this mind. Try to reach areas of intellectual capacity that you do not have but can obtain through a computer. Try to involve them to do things better than you can do yourself. Especially, when it comes to random processing where you can have things happen that you cannot even predict. That is the true essence of what a computer is. We should stop this whole idea that computers are inferior to human intellect, as if there is some sort of a competition going on, so as to prove to our colleagues that we are superior to the machine. It is ridiculous and should not even be happening.

Finally, I would like to offer an experiment that was established as a test of intelligence and is referred to as the Turing test. According to the experiment, if something, no matter what it is made out of, behaves convincingly as intelligent, then it is so. By definition. So, if a computer offers you a solution that involves an awe of intelligence maybe that is the case. In the original experiment, which is a theoretical one so far, a human converses with an entity that is hidden on the other side of a parapet without knowing whether it is another human, a computer, or something else. The point of the experiment is to detach the eyes from the form or connotation that is usually associated with intelligent beings; those could be non-human provided they pass the test. You do not know what you are talking to: it could be a human or a computer. You cannot see it. You cannot be influenced by the form, shape, or voice of your interlocutor. If intelligence is what you are seeking for then its container should be irrelevant.

So, that being said, I would like to offer a concluding remark: there is something remarkable going on and digital culture is emerging as a new prism of looking at the world asking us to redefine almost all of our established terms. This may be the biggest opportunity ever in the history of humanity so please do not miss it. I certainly am not. I love my computer and I think that it loves me too. A few days ago, while I was sleeping, deep in the calmness of the night, where everything was quiet, I woke up thinking that I heard a voice coming from my computer. It sounded like crying. It was a weak voice coming from inside my computer saying, "I want to be like you. Please be my friend. Please!"

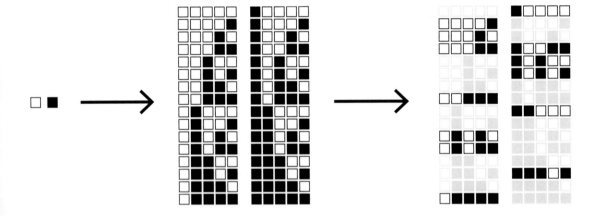

– 4 –

Combinations, Permutations, and Other Predicaments

A permutation is an ordered arrangement of the elements of a set. It is a rearrangement of elements in a different order to the original. For example, for a set of elements defined as {a, b, c, d}, the set {b, c, a, d} is one possible permutation. The term permutation is often used interchangeably either as a single ordering or as all possible orderings. In this text, we will use the first definition and, for all possible orderings, we will use the term *exhaustive* permutations.

Etymologically, the word permutation is derived from the Latin prefix per- which means through, along, or during and the suffix muto which means change or alter. In Greek the word for permutation is μετάθεσις, which, similarly, points to a process of change (i.e. μετα- means through and θέσις means position).

A permutation differs from but is often confused with a combination. While a combination is also a rearrangement of elements, in a combination the order of the arranged element within the set does not matter. For example, the order of fruits within the fruit salad {banana, apple, grapes} does not affect the set. In contrast, in a permutation the order of the arranged elements does matter such as in the case of a number lock where the order of numbers does have an affect over the set. For example, the number set 5674 for a number lock is very different from 7465 even though they both contain the same numbers. Incidentally, such locks are mistakenly called "combination" locks even though they should rather be called "permutation locks".

Within a set, it is possible that two or more permutations contain repetitive elements. For example, a lock can be opened using the sequence "2222" even though the number 2 is repeated four times. In contrast, there are cases where permutations cannot contain repetitive elements, such as the case of a race where two athletes cannot both be first at the same time.

A permutation is just one possible rearrangement of elements in a set. There can be multiple arrangements. In fact, the number of all possible arrangements can be estimated in advance using simple formulas. For a repetitive case, the number of possible permutations for a given set of n elements from which k elements are chosen can be estimated as:

$$p(n,k) = n^k \tag{1}$$

Similarly, for a non-repetitive case, the number of possible permutations for a given set of n elements from which k elements are chosen can be estimated as:

$$p(n,k) = \frac{n!}{(n-k)!} \tag{2}$$

where n! is a factorial. To illustrate the point, in Figure 4.1 an exhaustive list of all permutations of five colors arranged in a 2 × 2 grid is shown below (left). The number of permutations in this case is $5^4 = 625$. The same list is used again but this time only the non-repetitive arrangements are highlighted (right). The number of permutations now is 5!/(5–4)! = 120.

While the above formulas are quite useful for estimating the exact number of all possible permutations, they are not able to provide us with a visual display of how these permutations would look like (such as in Figure 4.1). In order to determine and generate the set of all permutations in a repetitive case we can use an algorithm such as the following (in Processing/Java/C):

```
1.   int n = 4;
2.   int k = 2;
3.   for(int i=0; i<pow(k,n); i++){
4.       print(nf((i+1),n) + " ");
5.       for(int j=0; j<n; j++){
6.           print((i/int(pow(k,n-j-1)))%k);
```

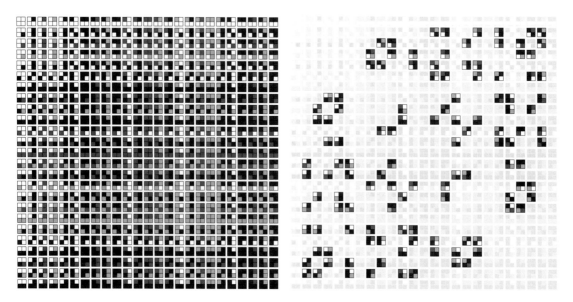

4.1 An exhaustive list of all permutations of five colors arranged in a 2 × 2 grid (left). The same list is used but only the non-repetitive arrangements are highlighted (right).

```
7.     }
8.        println();
9.     }
```

Specifically, in lines 1 and 2 of the code above, we define two integer variables: n for the number elements in the set and k for the number of chosen elements. Then we loop for the maximum number of all possible permutations (given by formula 1 above). Next, we loop for the number of elements and use the expression in line 6 to determine the sequence of elements in order to form the permutation. This algorithm generates all possible repetitive permutations of four elements taken two at a time and arranging them in a linear sequence as shown in Figure 4.2.

The permutations in Figure 4.2 are represented using numbers, specifically 0s and 1s. However, a permutation is an abstract ordering of a set and therefore can be represented by any data element; that is, in any shape, symbol, or form. Further, permutations can be represented linearly, i.e. as lying along a line or may be arranged in various different geometrical configurations, such as a circular or 2D/3D grid. In the example in Figure 4.3, we illustrate the permutations produced earlier of four elements taken two at a time as a series of squares or arranged in a 2×2 grid.

		(1)		(2)	(3)
01	0000	01	0000		
02	0001	02	0001		
03	0010	03	0010		
04	0011	04	0011		
05	0100	05	0100		
06	0101	06	0101		
07	0110	07	0110		
08	0111	08	0111		
09	1000	09	1000		
10	1001	10	1001		
11	1010	11	1010		
12	1011	12	1011		
13	1100	13	1100		
14	1101	14	1101		
15	1110	15	1110		
16	1111	16	1111		

4.2 Permutations of four elements taken two at a time allowing repetition. The number of all possible permutations is $2^4 = 16$

4.3 Permutations of four elements taken two at a time allowing repetition shown as binary numbers (column 1), along a line (column 2), and as a 2×2 grid (column 3)

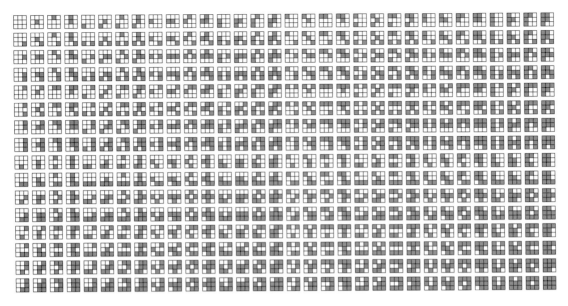

4.4 All possible permutations of nine elements arranged in a 3 × 3 grid, taken two at a time

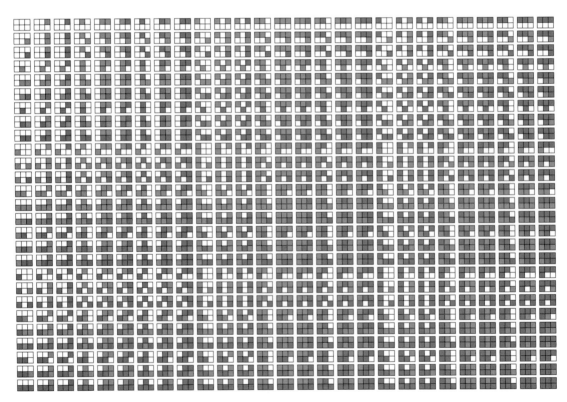

4.5 All possible permutations of six elements arranged in a 3 × 2 grid, taken three at a time

1. Geometrical Permutations

IN design, elements are often arranged on a grid; that is, a pattern of regularly spaced horizontal and vertical lines forming squares, which are used as a reference for locating points. Such grids could be regular, that is, consisting of equal distances or proportional. For the case of nine elements arranged in a 3 × 3 grid, taken two at a time, and allowing for repetition, the number of all possible permutations is $2^9 = 512$. An enumerated distribution (i.e. a list where there is a natural ascending ordering) of these permutations on a 16 × 32 grid is shown in Figures 4.4, 4.5, and 4.6.

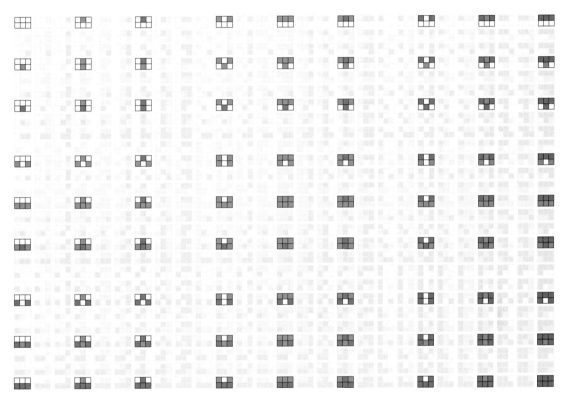

4.6 Symmetry constraint: the highlighted sets show only vertical symmetrical ones selected out of the pattern in Figure 4.5

Suppose, that we would like to find all possible permutations of a k elements taken from a set of n elements only once:

$$P(n,k) = \frac{n!}{k!(n-k)!} = \binom{n}{k} \tag{3}$$

The results of formula (3) can be seen in Figure 4.7 for n and k both as numbers and as patterns.

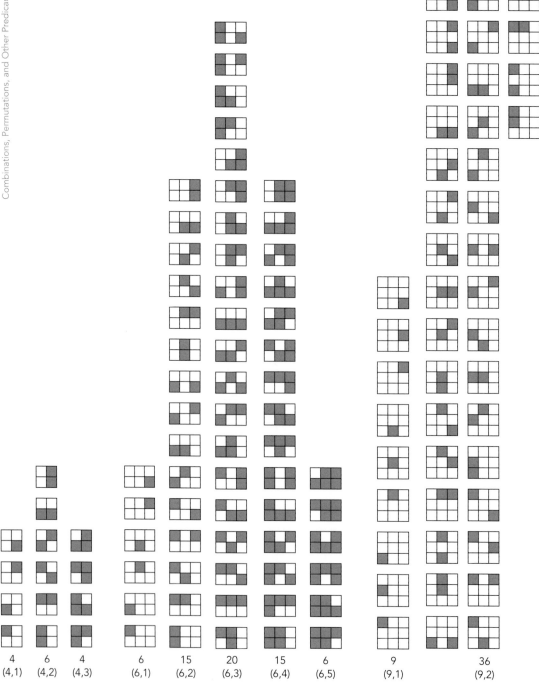

4.7 Various permutations for n and k based on formula (3)

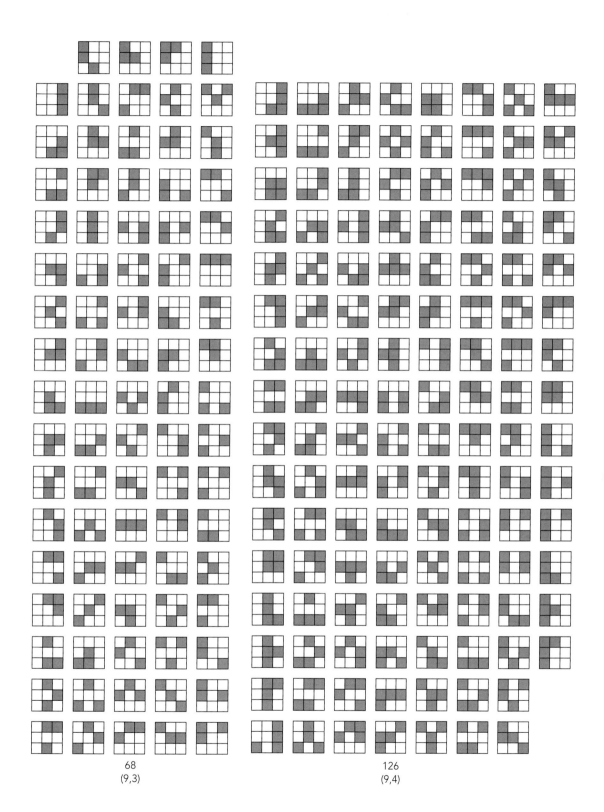

68
(9,3)

126
(9,4)

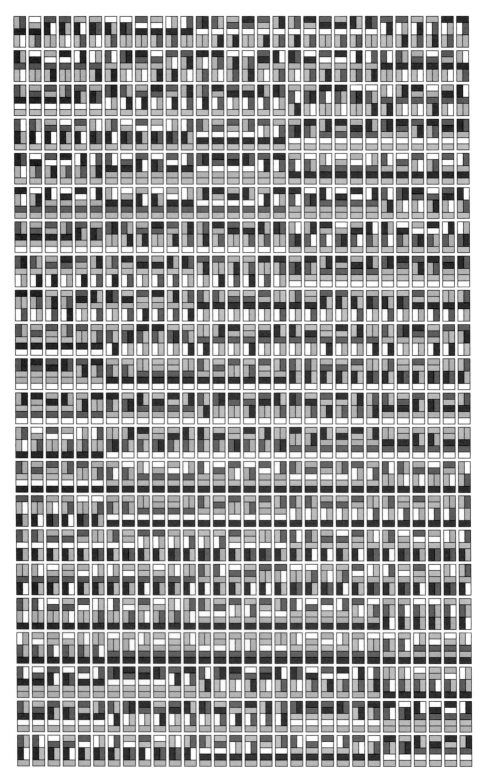

4.8 All possible permutations of five two-unit blocks in a 5 × 2 grid

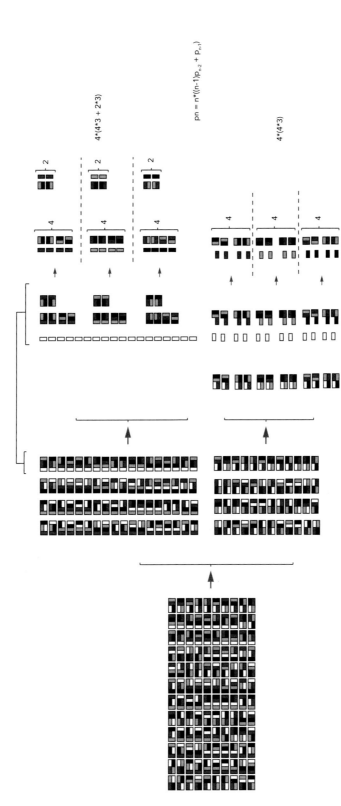

4.9 Analysis of all possible permutations of four two-unit blocks in a 4 × 2 grid

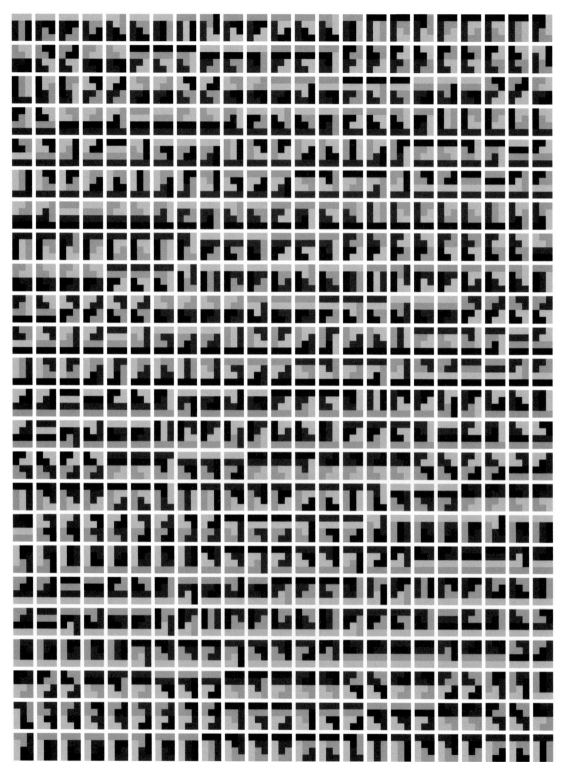

4.10 A table showing the exhaustive permutations of four colors, taken one-at-a-time, in contiguous blocks of three colors. The total number of permutations is 552 as indicated in Figure 4.5 at column 3 over row 12

Traditionally, the dominant mode for discussing permutations has been of a topological nature, where the arrangements of elements are assumed to be discrete and linear. The problem with this is that in design, arrangements are more complicated. In contrast, in design, permutations are defined by geometrical arrangements where shape and orientations matter (see Figures 4.8, 4.9, and 4.10).

2. Network Topology Permutations

A network topology is the ways in which a set of elements are interconnected. Each element will be referred to as a node and each connection as a link. So, for example, sets of nodes can be linked as shown in Figure 4.11.

Each of these networks assumes that each node is linked with every other one (also known as a complete graph). However, it is possible to link nodes in many different ways. Also, it is possible to find all the possible ways that a set of nodes can be connected (or not connected) with each other. For example, three nodes can be connected in eight possible ways, as shown in Figure 4.12.

As shown in Figure 4.12, each of the three nodes can be linked to two, one, or none of the other links in eight possible ways that are ordered in increments of links. In Figure 4.13, we show the case of four links where the possible connections are 64.

Let's try to determine a method that will allow us to pre-determine the number of all possible ways a number of n nodes can be linked. Let's construct a table where we can input the possibility of each link to be or not be linked to another one such as in the case shown in Figure 4.14.

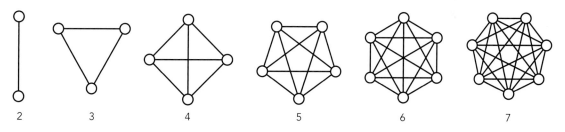

4.11 A network of two, three, four, five, six, and seven nodes where each node is linked with every other one

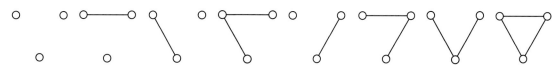

4.12 A network of three nodes and all possible ways they can be connected (in this case they are eight)

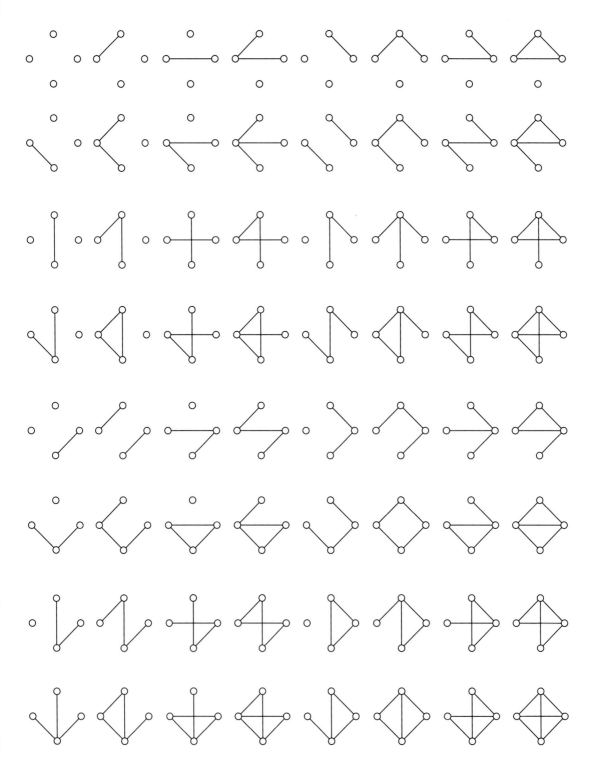

4.13 An 8 × 8 table containing all possible links (or lack thereof) of four nodes

	Node 1	Node 2	Node 3	Node 4	Node 5	Node 6
Node 1		0 or 1	0 or 1	0 or 1	0 or 1	0 or 1
Node 2			0 or 1	0 or 1	0 or 1	0 or 1
Node 3				0 or 1	0 or 1	0 or 1
Node 4					0 or 1	0 or 1
Node 5						0 or 1
Node 6						

4.14 A table representing possible link between six nodes

In Figure 4.14, we highlight only the cells that determine a possible link and we assign a value of 1 (for a link) and 0 (for the lack of a link). Notice that the diagonal black cells represent a self-link; that is, a link that starts from itself and ends in itself and those cells are omitted here. Also the lower part of the table (below the black cells) is also left empty because it represents the same information as that in the highlighted area (above the black cells). Either one can be used but not both.

So, the number of cells that represent possible links will be equal to the number of columns multiplied by the number of rows minus 1 and then divided by two. The reason is quite simple: we have an overall number of columns x rows cells but we leave out the self-links, so that amounts in one less column (or row). Since we need only the upper part of the table, we divide by two. But the number of columns will always be the same as the number of rows, so we can determine the number of cells we are looking for to be n(n-1)/2.

This number represents the number of possible links and since each link is defined to have a binary possibility, the number of possible connection of n nodes is:

$$P(n) = 2^{\frac{n(n-1)}{2}} \tag{3}$$

As evident in equation (1) above, the number of possible connections increases exponentially. Figures 4.15 and 4.16 show the number of nodes, links, and the possible connections that can be made.

Nodes	Links	Possible connections
2	1	2
3	3	8
4	6	64
5	10	1,024
6	15	32,768
7	21	2,097,152
8	28	268,435,456
9	36	68,719,476,736
10	45	35,184,372,088,832

4.15 A table representing the number of nodes, links, and possible connections for up to ten nodes

4.16 A 32 × 32 table containing all possible links (or lack thereof) of five nodes

In the next chapter, we will show the implementation of these formulas on large sets of geometrical, color, and architectural elements.

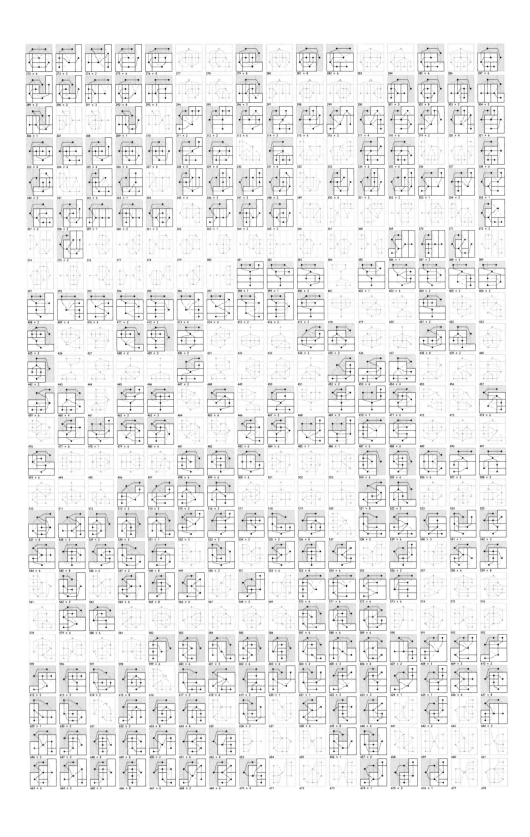

– 5 –
Studies

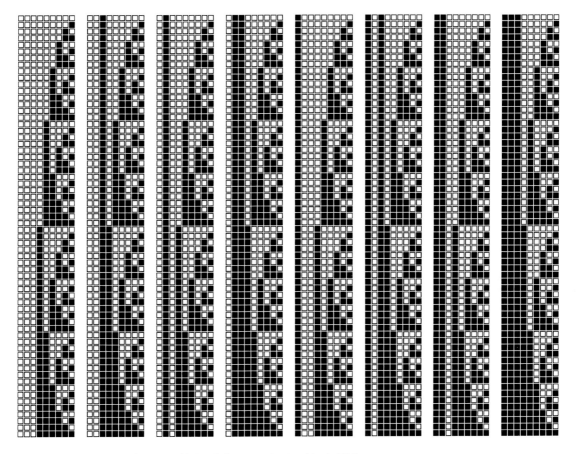

5.1 Exhaustive permutations of two colors (black and white) over a 9 × 1 grid (total of 512)

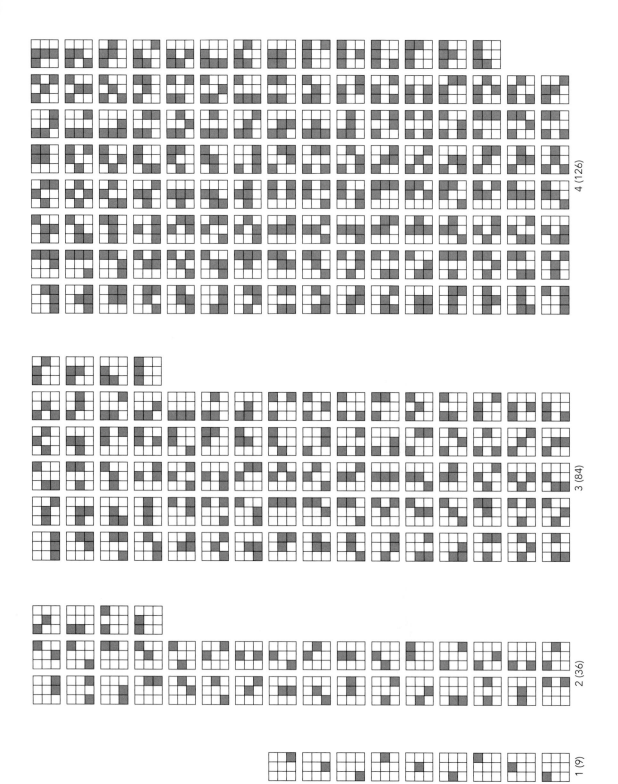

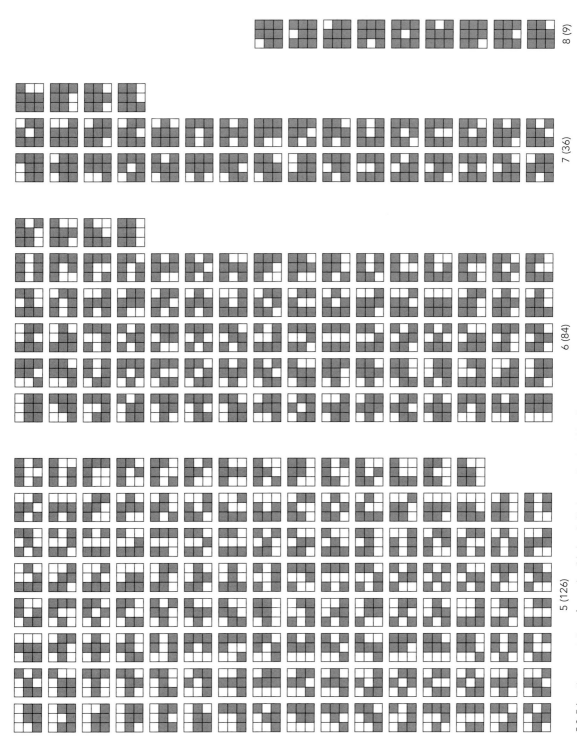

5.2 Exhaustive permutations of two colors (black and white) over a 3 × 3 grid (total)

Code in the Processing Language that Generates All Possible Permutations of Two Colors on a 3 × 3 Grid

```
import processing.pdf.*;
int n = 9;
int m = 3;
int l = 3;
int u = 8;
//size(n*10,(int)pow(2,n)*n*10);
void setup(){

  size(1100,800);
  beginRecord(PDF,"p"+m+"x"+l+".pdf");
  int bit = 0;
  for(int i=0; i<pow(2,n); i++){
    print((i+1) + " ");
    int j=0;
    for(int xx=0; xx<m; xx++){
      for(int yy=0; yy<l; yy++){
        bit = (i/int(pow(2,n-j-1)))%2;
        print(bit);
        if(bit==1)
          fill(100); //black
        else
          fill(255); //white
        rect(5+xx*u+(i/16*(m*u+8)),5+yy*u+((i%16)*(l*u+8)),u,u);
        j++;
      }
    }
    println();
  }
  endRecord();
}
void draw(){
}
```

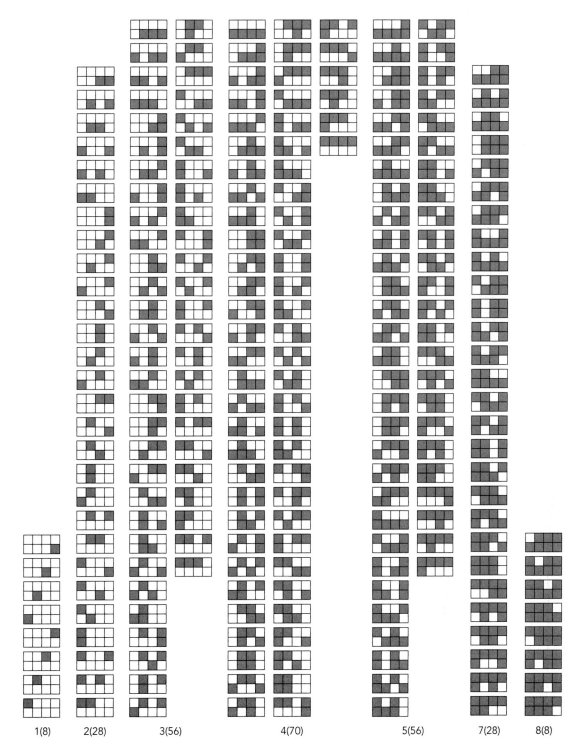

5.3 Exhaustive permutations of two colors (black and white) over a 4 × 2 grid

Studies **118**

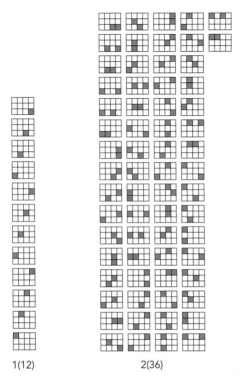

1(12)   2(36)

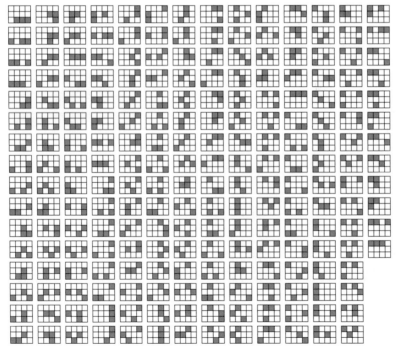

3(220)

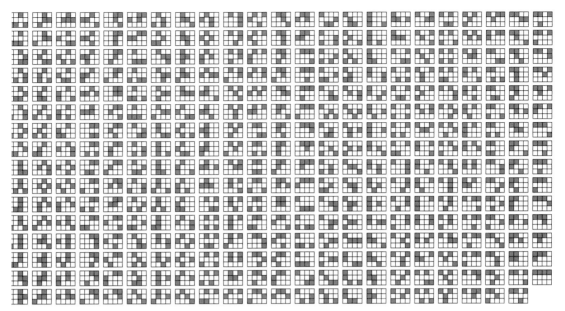

4(495)

5(792)

6(924)

5.4 Exhaustive permutations of two colors (black and white) over a 4 × 3 grid

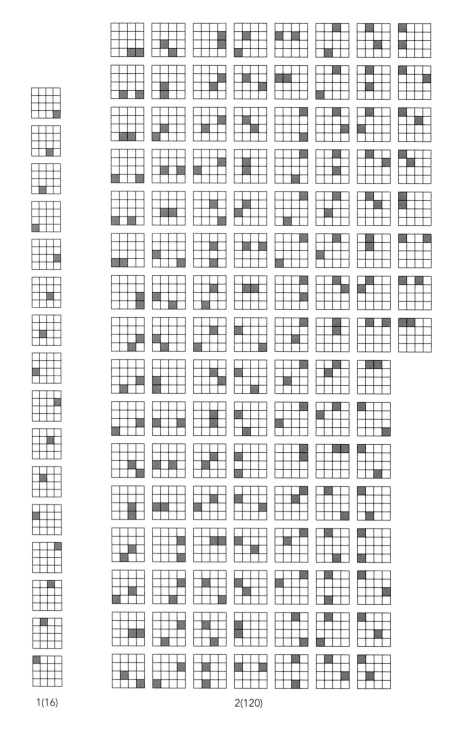

1(16) 2(120)

3(560)

4(1820)

5(4,368)

6(8,008)

7(11,440)

8(12,870)

9(11,440)

5.5 Exhaustive permutations of two colors (black and white) over a 4 × 4 grid

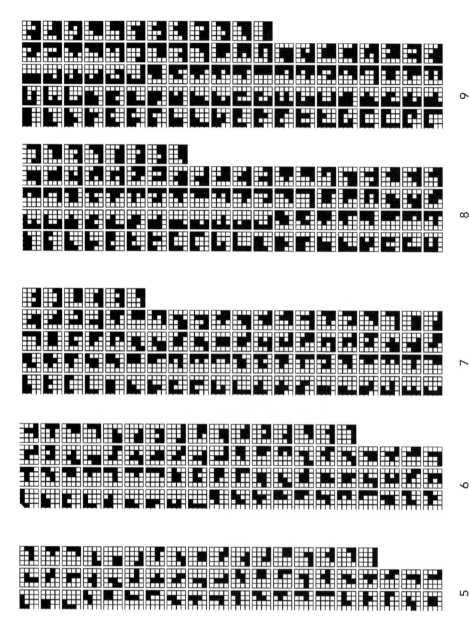

5.6 Permutations of two colors (black and white) over a 4 × 4 grid connected in four, five, six, seven, and eight contiguous blocks respectively

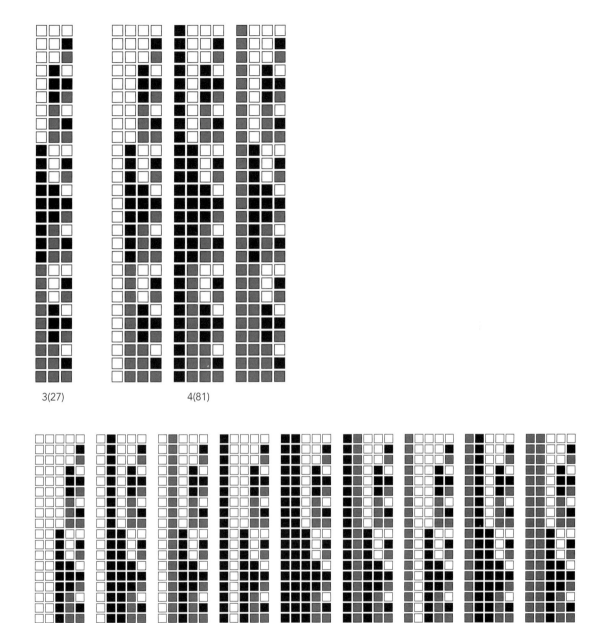

5.7 Exhaustive permutations of three colors (black, white, and grey) over a 3 × 1, 4 × 1, and 5 × 1 grids

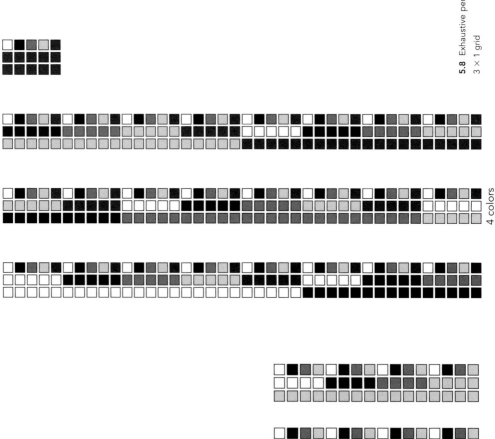

5.8 Exhaustive permutations of four and five colors over a 3 × 1 grid

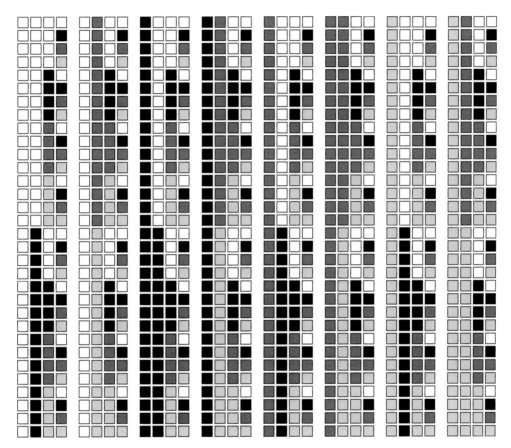

5.9 Exhaustive permutations of four colors over a 4 × 1 grid

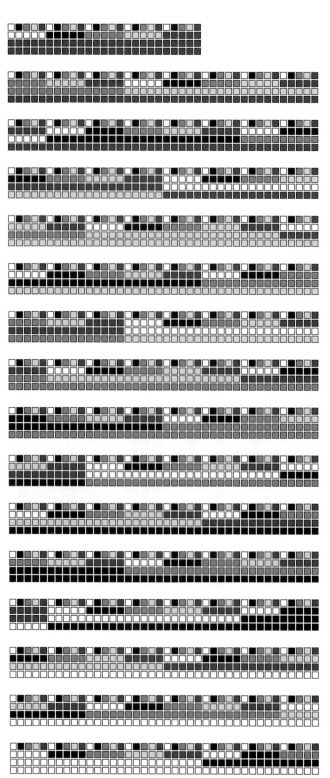

5.10 Exhaustive permutations of five colors over a 5 × 1 grid

Processing Code

```
import processing.pdf.*;
int n = 3;
int m = 4;
//size(n*10,(int)pow(2,n)*n*10);
void setup(){
  size(800,800);
  beginRecord(PDF,"p"+m+"_from_"+n+".pdf");
  int bit = 0;
  for(int i=0; i<pow(n,m); i++){
    print((i+1) + " ");
    for(int j=0; j<m; j++){
      bit = (i/int(pow(n,m-j-1)))%n;
      print(bit);
      if(bit==1)
        fill(0);        //black
      if(bit==0)
        fill(255);      //white
      if(bit==2)
        fill(255,0,0);
      if(bit==3)
        fill(0,255,0);
      if(bit==4)
        fill(0,0,255);
        rect(10+j*10 + (i/27*n*22),((i%27)*10)+10,8,8);
      //rect(10+j*10 + ((i/int(pow(n,m-1)))*n*12),((i%int(pow(n,m-1)))
      *10)+10,8,8);
    }
    println();
  }
  endRecord();
}
void draw(){
}
```

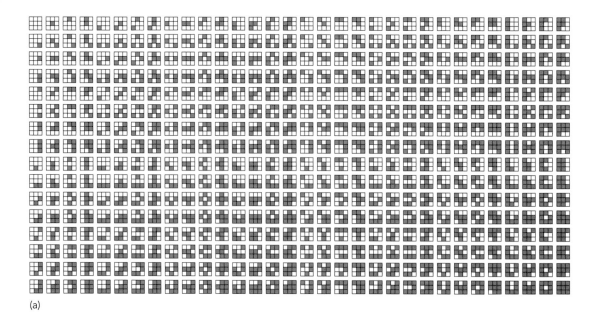
(a)

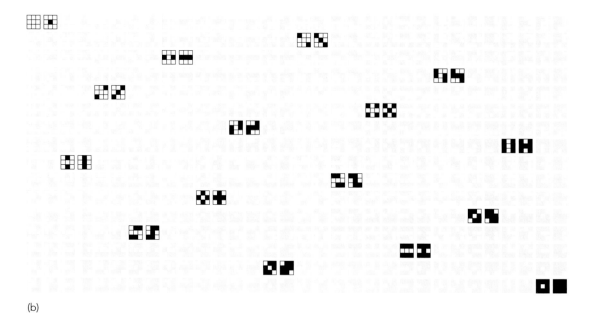
(b)

5.11 Exhaustive permutations of two colors on a 3 × 3 grid (a) and selection of all symmetrical cases (b)

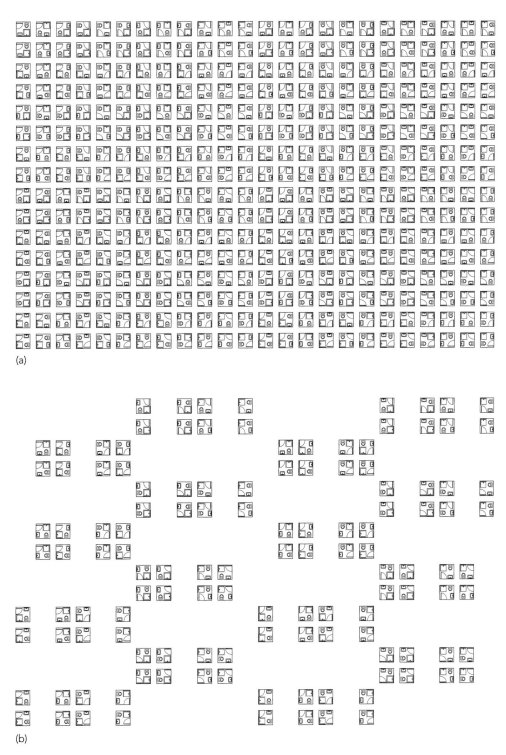

5.12 (a) Exhaustive permutations of four fixtures (sink, shower, toilet, and door) over a 2 × 2 grid; and (b) selected permutations where door does not open toward a toilet seat

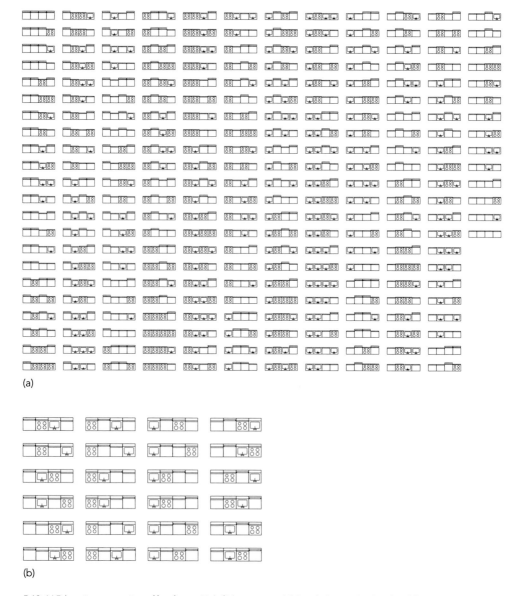

5.13 (a) Exhaustive permutations of four fixtures (sink, fridge, oven, and dishwasher) over a 4 × 1 grid; and (b) unique permutations of four fixtures (sink, fridge, oven, and dishwasher) over a 4 × 1 grid

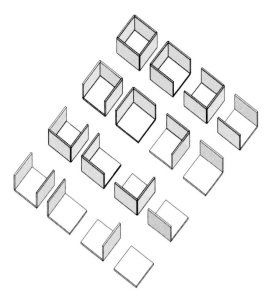

5.14 Exhaustive permutations of four walls

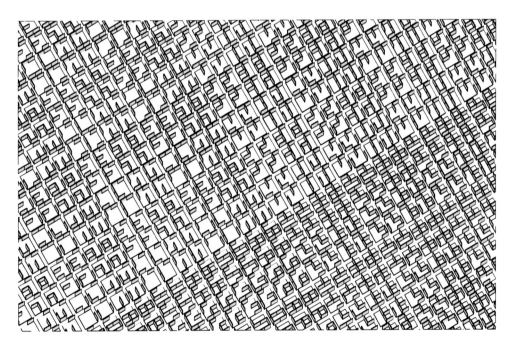

5.15 Exhaustive permutations of twelve walls in a 2 × 2 room configuration (partial view of 4,096 possible permutations)

MEL code

```
float $rp[];          //define a reference point
$n = 12;          // number of elements
string $s = "";          //string to strore the genome code
   for($i=0; $i<pow(2,$n); $i++){          //for all possible permutations
   $s = "";
      //print(($i+1) + " ");          // show the counter
      for($j=0; $j<$n; $j++){
         $s += ($i/int(pow(2,$n-$j-1)))%2;          //calculate the genome code
         }
      print($s + "\n");          //display the code
      $rp[0] = $j*5 + (($i/64)*5);          //get a x location
      $rp[1] = (($i%64)*5);          //get a y location
      $rp[2] = 0.;          //get a z location
      make4Walls2($rp, $s);
      }


// Procedure to draw twelve walls in a 2x2 room configuration
proc make4Walls2(float $rp[], string $gen){
polyCube;
scale 4 4 .1;
move 0 0 0;
move -r $rp[0] $rp[1] $rp[2];

for($i=0; $i<12; $i++){
//if the code is 0 do not draw a wall
   if(eval("substring \"" + $gen + "\" "+ ($i+1) + " " + ($i+1))
   =="0")continue;
   polyCube;
   if($i<6){
      scale .1 2 1;
      move (($i%3-1)*2) ((($i/3)%2*2)-1) .5;   //make a wall and place it in
                                               the right place
      }
   else{
      scale 2 .1 1;
      move ((($i/3)%2*2)-1) (($i%3-1)*2) .5;   //make a wall and place it in
                                               the right place
      }
   move -r $rp[0] $rp[1] $rp[2];   //place the whole pattern on a grand grid
   }
}
```

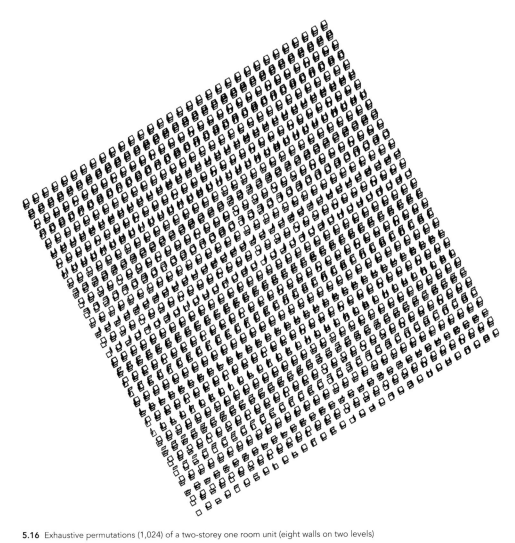

5.16 Exhaustive permutations (1,024) of a two-storey one room unit (eight walls on two levels)

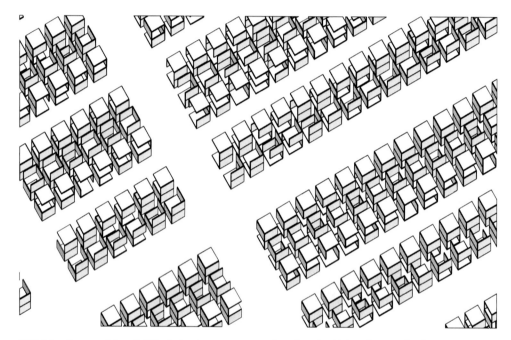

5.17 Exhaustive permutations (1,024) of a two-storey one room each configuration (eight walls on two levels) with constraint of gravity placed on a city grid (partial view)

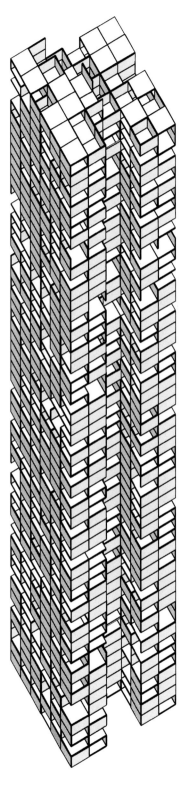

5.18 High-rise configuration of 1,024 2 × 2 × 2 rooms

5.19 The exhaustive permutations of walls in a 3 × 3 room plan are 224 = 16,777,216. See below a close view of all permutations

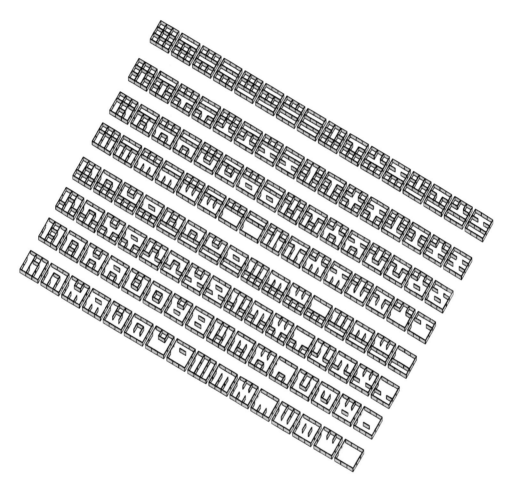

5.20 Constrained version of Figure 5.19. Here we set two constraints: full enclosure and y-axis symmetry. The possible plans are only 256 now

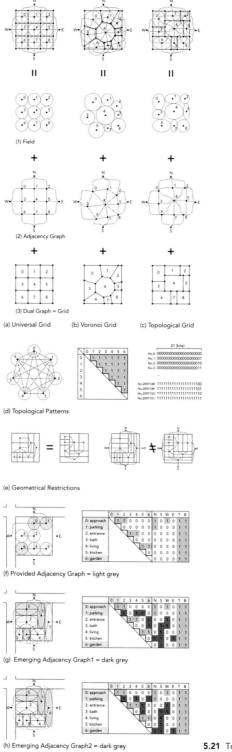

5.21 Topological grid

One algorithm can be used to generate a variety of grids. The grids are composed with the following three elements:

(1) Field

Space can be articulated with the functional units necessary for planning, as is done in Japan's nLDK system (a system for describing real estate, where L stands for living, D for dining, K for kitchen, and n for the number of additional rooms in a given property). In such a system, no distinction is made between interior and exterior. Here, we will refer to these articulated spaces as fields.

(2) Adjacency Graph

The use of a given field can change in a variety of ways depending on its adjacency relationships. Here, the connective relationships of a field are expressed as adjacency graphs.

(3) Dual Graph

Essentially, the dual graphs of adjacency graphs become grids. Floors, ceilings, walls, openings, and other architectural elements can be allocated based on dual graphs results to create design studies.

(d) Topological Patterns

Since adjacency relationships can be expressed using bits, the connective pattern of a field with n elements has a total of $2(n(n-1)/2))$ connection patterns. For example, for n=7, there are a total of 2.9 million topological adjacency relationships.

(e) Geometrical Restrictions

Supplying geometrical restrictions (e.g. directionality, the constraints of a rectangular site, the constraints of a single-storey building) to the results of n =7 reduces the possible grid patterns to 4,456, each of which is illustrated on the following pages.

(f) Provided Adjacency Graph

The results are inputted into a simple adjacency graph based on the designer's judgments.

(g) Emerging Adjacency Graph

Among the 4,456 patterns mentioned above, those that include the results of the (f) adjacency graph are depicted in color; 2,770 patterns satisfied the conditions.

(h) Emerging Adjacency Graph

In Figure 5.21 (g) and (h), the grids are the same, but the arrangements of the fields are different. The graphic representations of these types of variations are omitted from the following pages, but when n variations exist, it is indicated by an "x N" inscription. Including such variations results in a total of 16,920 grid patterns.

     If the adjacency relations predetermined by the designer (highlighted in light grey) ensure functionality and rationality, the new, emergent adjacency relationships (highlighted in dark grey) represent opportunities that yield variety and complexity.

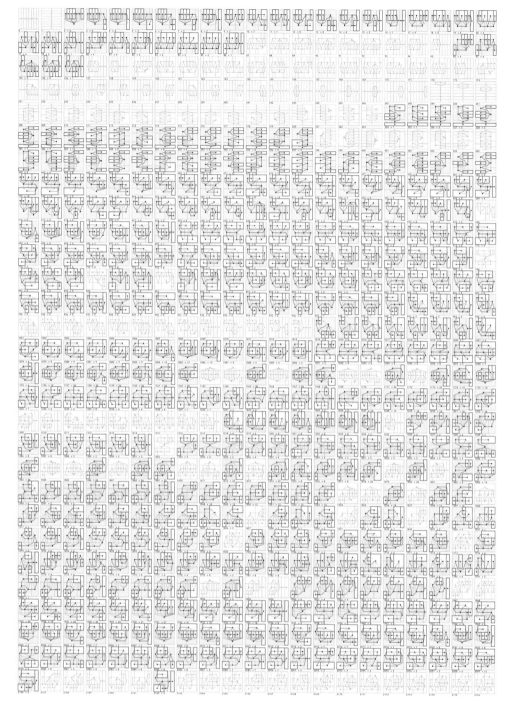

5.22 This system described in Fig 5.20 has the capability to generate a set of all possible permutations that oscillate between order and chaos. For instance, 26,8435,456 patterns of possible permutations can be generated from eight units of space. From the total number of such permutations, 32,512 may be selected based on geometrical conditions such as the grid to be rectangle, the orientation to be specific, and to be single-floored

Concurrently, the system will search the valid adjacency graph to match the relations given through a tree structure that is provided by the client/designer. In this case, 10,386 permutations were found acceptable from the 32,512 possible permutations (seen here as a partial view).

5.23 A series of spaces produced through the algorithm described in Figure 5.20, that represent a material version

Epi(dia)logue

NP: I can see in your work a tone of pessimism. As if the world of the author is ending. Some sort of "the death of the author". Is that true?

KT: Yes, I am talking about the death of the human author, yet that also implies the birth of another author, that of the nonhuman author. For every death there is a potential birth. Every generation is, hopefully, succeeded by the next generation. I think that the human generation, the way that we, at least, have conceived it in the last thousands of years, is changing dramatically and a new generation is being born which is made up of the author of authors; that is, the author of the authorship. In other words, the time has come that we will be able to make something that makes its own decisions. So, instead of us deciding what to say, we may be able to make something that will tell us about its own ideas. Consider a familiar example, such as that of a child: if I have a child and the child writes the story of its life, I as a parent certainly cannot take credit for that work. The same thing happens here as an author who develops software and the software makes the story for the author. In that sense you are the author of the software that makes the story; but not the author of the story. The story is not conceived by the human mind and manifested on a piece of paper directly but indirectly through another author. Somebody or something announces that this is what I think; this is what my opinion is, because this is who I am. So far, we are used to, within the humanistic/enlightenment paradigm, that such an announcement can only be made by a human being. But there is a new paradigm that involves the author as a composer of a device that creates the narration. The human author becomes a meta-author. In a way, you are an author of an author; that is, you make authors. You don't author yourself only.

DC: Considering the humanistic paradigm what do you think about trans-humanism? Is this a new religion? Is this our future to have something prosthetic in order to help us? Will this also help us in living or understand space?

KT: Prosthetic means that you are adding to something else. I am not talking about adding. Instead, I am talking about reinventing. Take, for instance, a mechanical pen instead of a pencil. Instead of pressing on the pencil, one can just touch the paper with a pen and it will still write; it becomes easier to write, but the idea of what to write is still in my mind. I still have to think and write with my pen regardless of its shape or softness.

Similarly, in the case of an artificial arm, it is still the mind that controls it. The question is whether you can extend your own mind. That is a different story altogether, which is what I am talking about here. So, an extension to the body assumes that the human mind still is the controlling agent; that is, the initiator of the movement through thought. Now, if I am going to create a story, I will have to come up with a series of thoughts, and then I need to use a typewriter or a pencil to express it and communicate it. That is an extension to my mind. Another example is running with artificial feet instead of my own; I am not talking about that. We already know that; it happens over and over in history. The question today is whether or not there is a way to extend the human mind; not necessarily replace it but rather extend it. If you are talking about the prosthetics to the brain or the prosthetics to the mind, then I am with you. Actually, I don't like the word brain; I prefer the word mind, which defines much more accurately the theoretical manifestation of the human organ called the brain.

So, if we consider the prosthetics of the mind then, by definition, we are referring to something beyond ourselves, because it means that we are extending our own self and consequently lose our ability to predict the results of our own actions. What I am trying to say is that if you have something that interferes with your own ability to make decisions, then that interference produces unpredictable to yourself results; such unpredictability affects in very profound ways your own authorship. To take it a little bit more close to your profession, an architect can be seen as an author; an author of forms, shapes, or materials. Instead of using letters, words, and phrases, the architect uses columns, walls, and other architectural elements in order to produce a story, which is the arrangement of these elements into a complete whole, resulting finally in the building itself. If the architect is the one that makes all the decisions, then the resulting product, the building, is by definition a predictable product of that mind. But if the mind is being altered in a prosthetic way, so as to deviate from the original intentions, then we get results that are not necessarily the predictable products of the author/architect. So, we would be talking about something else. I have given examples in my book, where I use my software, and at the end I make something that I never ever thought that I was going to get because of that interference. Because if I knew in advance what I was going to make, then I would have authorship of that product. But I don't, so then I will have to exclude my authorship. The problem then is who controls and therefore takes credit for the authorship. We still have a story (a novel or a building), perhaps, a brilliant one. I believe then that I have to give credit for authorship or part of my authorship to the device that helped me to do it. It is only fair. Is it not? So, in other words when you create a design, or manipulate an image with Photoshop and end up with a piece of art, then you also will end up with a piece of art that is not yours. I am sorry if you planned otherwise. . .

DC: We have surrealist artists who, at least, try to compete with that product done today more easily by the machines.

KT: Surrealism was the first step toward this sort of thing, except that surrealism was based on human-generated randomness. Even if you take drugs and lose control, or by intentionally using random methods, one cannot alter the result of what one is trying to do. Surrealist or

Dada work was in that realm. For example, Eugene Ionesco, the Romanian theatrical author, wrote all his short pieces or theatrical plays based on the predictability of the unpredictable. But he wrote everything himself. So, in a strange way, he predicted his own unpredictability.

Writing without having any connection with your conscious mind is something called automatic writing, and only afterwards one can attempt to explain it. Yet, there is a big difference from what is going on today. Today we have new kinds of methods that are electronic and implemented through computational techniques. Surrealists were the last authors in the sense of authoring unpredictable stories as opposed to incisions or prosthetics to the human mind that is what we have available today.

DC: Recently, I faced a problem in South Korea when I had asked three students to join me in a Chinese restaurant. They suddenly start to scan the public space with their smart phones in order to find one restaurant. Those made me think whether this will be the future for all of us in reading space.

KT: This is prosthetics again in the sense of adding more information to the visible world. The software is designed to enhance the ability to visualize extra information. But the reference point is always you, a human. Now suppose that the following happens: you go to a Chinese restaurant, and you pick ingredients such as mushrooms, onions, oyster sauce, etc. Then some software randomly puts these together and makes a food for you and it tastes so delightful like you never tasted anything like it before! Then that would be what I am talking about. That is neither an enhancement nor extra information, but a new recipe in the form of an algorithm that produces tasty food. And here is where it gets interesting: it is random so you don't have any access to the steps of the food making, because nobody did it for you. At the same time somehow it was done. In this case the question that arises is who made the food? Did you make it, because you press the button where it says "random"? No, because you didn't know how to make the food in the first place. On the other hand . . . Did the computer made it? No, it is not the computer who made it either. It is something else that is going on here that is what fascinates me: the birth of a strange alien authorship. It is also about the birth of a new chef, a "Chinese" chef in this case. We don't even know who this person is, doesn't have a face, doesn't have a hat, doesn't have a dress, and yet he or she or it has the ability to make food. It could be bad food or good depending on who tastes it, but still its creation is not predictable and it is not human-made; at least not in the sense that we are used to when we define something human. The word human in the last several thousand years is defined by assuming whatever we, the members of the human race, can think. But if we cannot think of something, then it doesn't mean that is not possible to exist. It just means that it is not by us. It is beyond us. So, that is the moment when the death of authorship as we knew it occurs.

DC: I remember from another conference in Crete that you had an optimistic ending/finish for your lecture.

KT: Yes, the word "death" is just a way to attract attention. Really, it is not about a death alone, because at the same time there is a birth, a continuation. It was just a catchy phrase (i.e. "the death of the author") so that some people may get interested, perhaps irritated, and then really come to the main point which is the birth of something else, or the transformation and extension of something into something new. And when I say new I mean it in a profound way. The interesting part is, of course, the birth, meaning that somehow we are able to overcome ourselves. And that new ability allows us to question ourselves in an existential or tautological manner because we are now in a position for the first time in history to doubt about the authority of our best abilities. In other words, we may not be as good as we think we are. The best Chinese cooker may not be as good as a random cooker.

DC: I would like you to explain what the difference between algorithmic and parametric is, and if it is the same as the difference between science and technology. When science invents something new it is a revolution, when technologies invent something new it is just a little step.

KT: The first to observe is the difference between algorithmic and parametric from a linguistic point of view. Both words sound like Greek words but the first one is Arabic and only the second Greek. But that is not important. An algorithm is basically a way of addressing a problem. If it is solvable, then these steps lead toward solving the problem. However, we are not always confronted with problems that have a solution. So, it is more accurate to say that an algorithm is the series of steps that one takes in confronting a problem. Of course, one such problem could be a parametric one. There is a misconception about the word parametric. Theoretically, in mathematics, parametric is a relationship made out of variables, each one affecting the other one, in a balancing manner. Take, for example, an equation that is parametric. That means that it contains variables called parameters that if you increase one, then the other one or ones will decrease. It is a balancing act. The word parametric has been used apparently in architecture as a design methodology for solving formal problems that architects may have, or at least that is how it has been presented. So, the way that they do it is by taking the parameters that describe a form and increase or decrease their quantitative levels; that is, their parameters. So, if you take a surface and regard it as formal representation based on parameters (i.e. the parametric equation of a surface), that means that if you increase one parameter then that act will have an effect in the form, and if you decrease another one then that will have another effect, and so on. In that sense, the designer can play with parameters by increasing and decreasing them to produce different forms. That is the formalistic version of parametric, and because that representation is available through computational schemes to be materialized into building elements it had a great effect in architecture. By definition parametric is algorithmic because in order to make a parametric equation you will have to follow a series of steps manually or computationally. In a way, algorithmic is a higher category that contains parametric. Parametric is an implementation of an algorithm. In my opinion, the way that parametric is being used right now is very superficial, because it doesn't have the depth or the mathematical rigor that it should have amongst architects.

Personally, I lost my interest in that kind of work a long time ago. All I see is blobs, strange shapes, and forms; some of them are not even functional, let alone livable spaces. They all seek supposedly to address beauty but, in the name of it, they lose their architectural identity by becoming mere sculptural forms. In that sense I don't think parametric does contribute to architecture as it could. Quite the opposite, I think it degrades the value of architecture because it promotes buildings that are superficial and not livable, let alone disorients the designers.

DC: Most of the architectural experiment right now all over the world is in parametric architecture. They face the problem on how to build them. Some of them are cases of enveloping spaces and like this look like architecture, or works of art. How will these parametric algorithms help us in the future?

KT: Like I said earlier, if parametricism was used in the true and profound sense, then it could be useful. But it wasn't. By definition, architecture is parametric in the sense that it has to adjust its form in order to fit into a particular site and fulfill particular needs/parameters. So, if you want to adjust the form of a room, given a particular set of constraints, then you have to push and pull the room's shape by reducing something in one part and increasing something in another. But when it becomes parametric in the sense of software-based parametric then we have a problem. Architects buy or use software that is based on mathematical parametric equations such as nurbs and through the software the architect is given handles to push and pull affecting parameters of the equation. But when this action is only superficial, that is, used only to make a sculptural form, then we have a problem. At least, I have a problem because that is not really addressing the actual issues of architecture such as function, space, or performance. Instead it uses the software as a formal lab and it stops there after making sculptural elements. The process is formalistic and superficial and I don't believe in it; other people love it. I am not one of them. I am more interested in deeper levels of architectural manifestation and the roots of spatial composition. So, I agree with you but only if software is used correctly, parametrically speaking. I am more interested in the overall parameters that are part of architecture, not the formal issues alone.

DC: This envelope could be seen from outside or from inside, could also have a space of its own, and could use a technology. Architecture has a form, a function, significance, and as you have said before performance. Most of this performance in the buildings is visible on the envelope level. The design for these envelopes could also help the public space by being interactive and activate as a media facade. What do you think could be the possible direction on this problematic?

KT: The performance itself could be driven by software. My problem is in the use of the formal element in the software world. The software that is used by architects is software that is not made by architects. Therefore, the issue of performance, form making, or function is not architectural, *because it is not made by the architects themselves*. So, in principle I agree with you that the parametric may have a positive effect in architecture but only theoretically speaking. Practically, when it is used through software that is not under the architects' control, then we have the following problem: you don't know how they work, you don't know what they do, you have never done it yourself and that becomes very dangerous, because it becomes very superficial. Let me take the case of performance. You may "experiment" with form, and by pressing buttons you may produce a curvy surface that you like.

The problem is that you don't have the knowledge of how the form was produced. The software gave the form to you. If you had the ability to write your own software or, even better, if you had the ability to write software that produces forms based on hundreds of other parameters, then you would be producing something new, something that would be parametrically correct in my opinion. But the problem is that they are not doing that. They are simply following the software that was given to them by some other industry, and try to do building with it. There are two risks here. First, they are unaware of what is going on. They are not in charge. They don't know what is going on internally. Second, they cannot inject into the system multiple parameters, including random factors to produce something that is different and potentially better than the previous. In my work, I emphasized the idea of permutations, among others, which is a mathematical rearrangement of elements in a group. By doing billions or trillions of permutations you may come up with one, which may solve your problem much better than what you would have done on your own. That is another added feature that you don't have in the software-based parametric world. Especially when you are using other people's software. Sometimes scripting languages are useful but they are also constrained by the software that they reside in. So, in that sense again you are limited by the bounds of the software limiting in turn your own means of expression. By writing your own software, writing your own code, you can inject ideas into the program and take advantage of computational complexity that the computer allows you to. That is something that we are not taking advantage of. We could have, but for the time being we are not.

DC: Have you tried to develop such software?

KT: I have developed many such pieces of software. They are related to various mathematical, physical, or biological methods. Specifically, the permutation-based is the one software that comes from me and it is appropriate for architecture. In the past, I had experimented with biological processes, such as cellular automata. They are not architectural. They are more appropriate to describe living organisms or social networks. Or, take morphing: morphing is the transition of one shape into another and the production of in-between shapes but at the same time it is a formal technique that is not architectural. Architecture, in my opinion, resembles a puzzle with pieces where trying to put them together is the problem. Nothing comes from nowhere and nothing vanishes into nothing. So in that sense the permutation methodology addresses this issue of puzzle solving by taking the pieces of the puzzle that pre-exist and rearranging them in all possible ways using extreme calculations and producing all possible patterns until it hits the best one. I think that the software that I am developing is more appropriate for architecture. Also, I used the same software for the generation of text in a true DADA futuristic manner. I took the permutations of words and I produced sentences and then paragraphs and then stories. And, strangely, these stories are very interesting. That is something that in my opinion is futuristic. That is where the future is. That will be my contribution.

DC: I find very interesting your conferences on Critical Digital. How was your last conference named ALGODE in Japan? Has it added something new to your theory?

KT: The conference we organized in Japan used the prefix ALGO, which is short for algorithmic because the Japanese could not pronounce it well and the suffix DE, which stands for design. That is how the word ALGODE came up. But in Greek the word *ALGODE* (ἀλγωδεία) means pain of music; that is, the song of pain. And then I realized something important: if there is pain then there is a patient. And if there is a patient then there should be a doctor. So, if there is a patient–doctor relationship in the algorithmic world, then I have to ask myself who is the patient and who is the doctor. I realized by using hidden code built into the Greek language that patient is the designer and doctor is the software developer, who actually helps the patient to make design, because they need a doctor.

In other words, whoever claims to be a big designer may only just be the patient in a world where they need a doctor to help them. Once they find a doctor who prescribes software such as Maya, or Rhino, they become well. That means that the true designers are the software designers, which in any point could stop prescribing the medicine and then the patient will die. Or they could give them placebos, like they already do now, and they will think that they are doing design, but really they are not. At ALGODE this possibility was developed into a conversation regarding who is the doctor and who is the patient. The word ALGODE was the code name of the medicine.

We are suffering from a post-humanistic misconception that still wants us to believe that the human world is run by geniuses, but it is not like that any more. There is no such thing as a genius. As a matter of fact if there is a genius I will ask that person to come forward and talk to me. I am still looking for one but I have never found any. I've heard about them. But that is not enough. As a professor in one of the best schools in the world, shouldn't I run into at least one genius? In the same sense, I am forced to believe that none of the so-called great architects is a genius either. They are all limited. We are limited. Everyone is limited. Even if you are called "genius" it is only a name, an epithet. Yet, by using computation some of the designers take advantage, but that does not mean that they should take full credit since their findings were based on the software developers' work. In a humoristic manner that was the conclusion of the ALGODE conference and that became a manifesto of the patient–doctor relationship. Somebody needs to break out the news sooner or later. The sad part is that students hope they can become geniuses of architecture and schools of architecture don't train students to develop software, which is the only way that they come closer to their "genius" dream. Instead they give them false hopes.

DM: I think of one cultural thing left out from your book and I would like to discuss it. During the golden days of modernism humanity experienced a whole series of nostalgia, not in the sense of the prairie house. Even postmodernism was a kind of nostalgia, such as the return to painting or sculpture. So, my question is whether you think that we may one day return also to a kind of digital nostalgia for things such as materiality or style. Because by looking at your work I see a lack of style and character. Of course, randomness can replace style but how about nostalgia?

KT: Very nice question. I would like to point out the difference between process and target. If nostalgia is pointed toward the target (i.e. the building), then maybe it is pointed at the wrong direction. Maybe what is interesting in the whole concept of style is not the final product but the process; the software that produces the digital object, not the result that came out of it. So, in the future, the memory of style will not be the digital outputs but the computer software that was used at that time so that the designers could accomplish their products, in a "meta design" fashion, that is, the style of a "process of a process"; in this case it would be the "design of design". In a strange way, style is not in the screen that you are looking at but in the code that was written. Right inside the device. So, in my opinion, style would be defined in how people used the computer to design not in the things they made which, by the way, were many, diverse, and abundant. Even today we are still nostalgic about the Maya period and I do not mean the Central American culture but the computer program called Maya that was a determinant factor of style back in the early 2000s.

VT: Why did you leave the word "inspiration" out of your work?

KT: I didn't. In fact, I tried to make it the central theme of this lecture by trying to replace it. I tried to replace what we hold as dear; that is, the essence of our humanity demonstrated through our inspiration. The idea that I can be the designer, the idea that I can change the world with my idea. I, as a designer, creator, can make a difference with my ideas. That is the idea behind inspiration. And what I am trying to say is that even that, which we hold as the most valuable, the most important thing that defines our destiny and our identity, even that can be replaced. In fact, that is what I was trying to prove in this book, not in the mathematical sense of a full-blown proof but rather give the seeds of something that could deny that privilege. By the way, I have nothing against inspiration; as a matter of fact, every piece of software that I write comes from inspiration but I try to take that inspiration and objectify it, if you like, and put it in the context of an inspiration of inspiration, or a meta-inspiration because I am inspired to destroy inspiration. That is inspiration in a kind of twisted way: if I want to destroy inspiration I need to be inspired to do so too. Right? But again I need to emphasize the importance of words and their meaning. When I say inspiration I mean something else and that is where the whole argument becomes interesting because once we get into the twists of the words, we enter into a world of agreement or disagreement based on our common definitions. Maybe that is why I like English because to me it is not loaded with connotations as opposed to Greek, my native language, and so I can see the world differently. I bet that if I translated verbatim this whole book in Greek, which I can, it would be understood in a whole different way.

PP: Kostas, your comments alone would be the topic of another book. I agree with many things that you say but for the sake of argument I will concentrate on one that I disagree with. My question is how one defines a good design. I think that there is no best design solution but always a better one. So, out of millions of solutions according to you we can get the best solution quantitatively but what if we want a better solution qualitatively? Then we are stuck.

KT: I have no disagreement. The only argument that I would make to contrast this is in the notion of design evaluation itself that I think is where the misunderstanding is happening. Why something is better than something else is ultimately left to the opinion of the so-called experts at least in the world of "high architecture". That is not true though for the common layman who produces architecture. There, best is the most efficient, functional, and inexpensive. So, in that world, if you objectify quantitatively what good is, then the computer is your friend. A computer can process a solution that will meet your needs in the best possible way. Think of the toilet example earlier, an ironic one, yet a very true one. If you respect the rules then yes you do have the best toilet. And, trust me, you will need it. In fact, there is no better (or should I say optimal) solution than the one composed by the computer since it went through all possible ones and found only that one. I am not interested in the competition-based jury teams because they define "good architecture" as an everlasting vague ambivalent condition that ultimately has to satisfy some people-experts that I am not even sure whether they are worth such an honor. So, that is not of interest to me. I am interested in the 99% of the rest of architecture that is done every day, everywhere, and from everybody. A week ago, I was on a Greek island. As I was walking in those magnificent settlements I could not help seeing permutations everywhere: all possible combinations of materials in all different ways but ultimately based on optimal selection. Any break of the rules would mean extra labor, sweat, and money. But any alteration of the rules could fit optimally within the general spirit. I frankly do not think that the anonymous native builder proposes a break of the rules to the client but rather an alternative permutation that fits into the logic of both the builder and the client.

PP: How do you regard mistakes? Do we need them?

KT: We need unpredictable actions. These are not necessarily mistakes. A mistake involves intentionality such as breaking a rule intentionally, but I am interested in the unintentional shift of expectation where something occurs without my consent and yet leads to a satisfying possibility. That I like.

GS: I have three points to make. First, you have conveyed a great skepticism about design and computation and so I am wondering about the politics behind software. Second, I would like to ask you your opinion about computer languages and their role in design. And the third question has to do with typology and how you see types that lack cultural meaning.

KT: The politics of software control is not done by politicians/architects but by software companies that decide in advance for you, usually without you. Consider that most software packages were not done by designers but by computer scientists or engineers that knew little, if anything, about design itself. And yet these people have the power to control your way of rendering, fabricating, drafting, and ultimately designing. As of language, in your second question, let me define what a computer language is: it is a communication medium between a human and a computer. The difference between human languages and computer languages is that one of the two parties is not human. That brings a whole new perspective to the problems of linguistics, not only in its methods but mainly in its own existence. Who are we speaking to? Is it the machine or ourselves to be reflected through the communication? I believe in the latter position. So, if you look into the computer languages they are usually in English, and for a good reason since they were invented in English-speaking countries. So, as far as communicating from a user's point of view it must be in English. However, that is of least complexity when communicating with a computer. The essence of the language lies in the syntax used and that is where the human communication skills become important. By using syntax the same problem or question can be articulated in different ways making your personal choices of communication very essential. So, a person who has a problem to solve though a computer may structure the algorithm in completely different ways, each of which reflects that person's thinking. But it doesn't end there. It gets much more complex to communicate because on the other side of the "conversation" there is a non-human agent. Of course, the lower you get into language structures the more possibilities for communication you have with a computer; which is the opposite for humans. The less you use predefined packages, offered to you by software vendors, the freer you are. I tend to use a metaphor of a swimming pool. If you use the scripting languages provided by software applications, you are limited by the software application's possibilities. It is like swimming in a swimming pool. You can go wherever you want but within the limits of the pool. Of course, for the software applications this is desirable because then you not only use their software but you are unable to use any other one. Now, once you start writing your own code then you get into a lake. And if you have access to hardware and low-level language structures you are in the ocean. All vendors want to control is your thoughts and your money as a commodity-based business. I do not blame them for that. I blame those who fall into the trap and instead of confronting their limitations they celebrate them instead.

Now, as far as architecture is concerned I hate to tell you but these "evil" computer programmers call themselves also architects. But of a different kind: they are abstract typologists that create methods of addressing problems. They see a type not as the resulting form with some cultural meaning attached to it, but rather as a process of building up thoughts. So, in my case as a software architect, I produce a permutation-based system that results into abstract geometrical or topological types: you see a U-shape, a T-shape, an O-shape all of them, everywhere, ever. I got types resulting from 4-squares, 9-squares, 16-squares. I bet great and radical architects would love to be able to do this but I am afraid they cannot. Not because they cannot think of it, no, I am sure that they can think much deeper than I can when it comes to traditional geometry, culture, or linguistics. They may be algorithmic. They may be able to methodically address any problem. They just don't know how to program and that is their limitation, because it is one thing to surprise other people and another thing to surprise yourself. What do I mean by that? Writing computer code requires fantasy, skills, and knowledge but the results that you get may surprise you in the most fundamental way. You may find out that you were right but you may also find that you are wrong; proven wrong. And that is a success beyond the failure. Unfortunately, there is no way to find out if you do not send the problem to a computer to see the results; over and over. Learning every time how wrong (or right) you were and shaping a new path that you would have never ever imagined. That interaction is what computers offer to architecture and to humanity in general.

DT: Your approach is quite interesting but it lacks the humanistic side. Where is the ancient Greek value of "know thyself"?

KT: Strange, because I thought that the message that the Greeks sent to the world was the exact opposite: to exceed theyself. Do you remember the myth of Peleas and Thetis? Of course, in order to exceed oneself, one needs to know oneself. But that is not enough. That is not the final objective. Exceeding oneself is far more difficult, but far more beneficiary. To exceed oneself, one needs to think differently, perhaps, the opposite way. Because if you think the way you always do, then you will be limited by acting within the same thought pattern. Take the example of the puzzle. There are many different ways to solve a puzzle, but always one uses the same thought pattern: trying to be smart. Exhaustive permutations are not intelligent. In fact, they are the exact opposite: mindless and idiotic.[1] But collectively, they produce an "intelligent" result. A companion in this process is the computer. A device, analogical to the human mind albeit not the same, allows humans to explore possibilities that were impossible before. But the computer alone is not enough. We have to think differently. It is up to us to come up with ideas that challenge the basic beliefs that we grew up with. And then we will learn about ourselves by viewing ourselves from beyond us. And I use the word "viewing" here, not in the English sense of visual observation, but in the Greek sense of self-reflection. The word "Goddess" (ΘΕΑ prn "Thea") and the word "view" (ΘΕΑ prn "thea") have the same root. Why? Think about it.

DT: From your work it seems to me that programming is a religion to you. What are your thoughts on that?

KT: Programming is a way of conceiving and embracing the unknown. At its very best, programming goes beyond developing commercial applications. It becomes a way of exploring and mapping our own way of thinking. It is the means by which one can extend and experiment with rules, principles, and outcomes of traditionally defined design processes.

In developing computer programs, the programmer has to question how people think and how mental processes develop and to extend them into real dimensions through the aid of the computers. In other words, computers should be acknowledged not only as machines for imitating and appropriating what is understood, but also as vehicles for exploring and visualizing what is not understood. The entire sequence of specifying computer operations is similar (albeit not equal) to that of the human thinking. When designing software, one is actually transferring processes of human thinking to a machine. The computer becomes a mirror of the human mind, and as such, reflects its thinking.

A few weeks ago I was at a conference that investigated the future of computers in architecture. I had expected that the panelists would address the opportunities presented to architects and designers alike by the advances in computer-aided research. Instead, most everyone seemed interested exploring existing programs, as opposed to holding a philosophical position driven by their own concepts. At that time I asked a question to a panel of experts about the necessity of designers to know how to program computer code. The answers that I got from them were very surprising to me, ranging from "what does programming have to do with design?" to "yes, design applications should be customizable". At that point I realized that the question should have been "how much programming should the designer know?"

You may already have deduced that I do think that programming is an important part of design education and practice. Programming involves more than simple problem solving, because it is the only way to use the computer to its full capacity, and for challenging known facts. Programming is the vehicle for obtaining new knowledge, for seeing things that cannot be seen, and for taking your fate, as a designer and architect, in your own hands.

Let me give you an example of a personal experience. This example deals with the very basics of architecture: perspective and three-dimensionality. As we all know, any CAD program will allow the designer/architect to project into space any object/point, and will be able to render it accurately, as long as the designer/architect does not challenge the very basis of the architectural projection: that of a projection being always bound to a formula of positive numbers. For example, the mathematical formula for a perspective projection is $f(x,y,z)=(x^*t, y^*t)$ where $t = d + d/z$ and d is the distance of the user to the projection surface. What if I give d a negative value? Can you imagine what that would look like? Can you draw the result on a piece of paper? it is just a simple formula now, isn't it? Do you know of any CAD application that would allow you to mess around with the perspective projection? I doubt you would find any such application unless somebody gives you the application's code for you to change. But that would involve two things: the designer/architect knowing how to program and the developers giving them the code.

In reality, there is an unraveling relationship between the needs of a designer/architect and the ability of a specific program to address these needs at all times. This can be attributed to a number of factors. First, designers are never really taught how to program (one needs to look no further than the question/answer "what does programming have to do with design?"). Schools do teach students how to use CAD tools, how to play around with applications, but they do not adventure into teaching the language, structure, philosophy, and power of programming.

Second, CAD developers rarely release code. You will be asked what you want, you will be offered interfaces for customization but you will not be given access to the code. For good reasons, code is proprietary information, and information is power. So, if a designer/architect wants to mess with the perspective formulas, they will need to write the modeling, interface, display, optimization, and debugging modules on their own. How many people who either have the time or the know-how to do this do you know? When are we going to see a Linux-like CAD system? When are we going to start a community of designers/architects/programmers sharing common code, for the advancement of CAD?

I tend to believe that today a designer's creativity is limited by the very same programs that are supposed to free their imagination. There is a finite amount of ideas that a brain can imagine or produce by using a CAD application. If designer/architect doesn't find the tool/icon that they want they just can't translate that idea into form. And whenever they see a new icon (let's say "meta-balls") they think they are now able to do something cool. But are they really doing anything new? If a designer knew the mathematical principles and some of the programming behind the newest effects, they would be empowered to always keep expanding their knowledge and scholarship by always devising solutions untackled by anybody else. By using a conventional program, and always relying on its design possibilities, the designer/architect's work is sooner or later at risk of being grossly imitated by lesser-devised solutions. By cluttering the field with imitations of a particular designer's style, one runs the risk of being associated not with the cutting-edge research, but with a mannerism of architectural style.

In this light, there are many designers claiming to use the computer to design. But are they really creating a new design? Or are they just rearranging existing information within a domain set by the programmer? If it is the programmer who is asking first all the questions, then who is really setting the parameters and the outcome of a good design? We saw already the I-Generation (Internet-Generation). When are we going to see the C-Generation, that is, the Code-Generation, the generation of designers/architects that can take its fate into their own hands . . . ?

Note

1. In English, the word idiot is derived from the Greek word διώτης which means private (i.e. doing things on your own). In turn, the word ἰδιώτης is derived from the word ἴδιος which means "the same", derived, in turn, from the word δεῖν, which means "to see" (which is where ideas come from).

– INDEX –

adaptive, 5

Alexander, 4, 14, 33, 35

ALGODE, 150, 151

algorithm, 2, 3, 4, 5, 10, 11, 12, 24, 26, 27, 30, 33, 34, 65, 66, 69, 73, 76, 78, 85, 86, 88, 90, 99, 100, 148, 149, 150, 155

alphabet, 40, 42, 43

ambiguous, 34, 37, 47

apprehend, 54

architecture, 1, 2, 13, 14, 17, 27, 30, 33, 35, 50, 65, 66, 67, 69, 149, 150, 151, 152, 153, 154, 155, 156, 157

arithmetic, 2, 19, 20

art, 1, 3, 7, 14, 34, 35, 50, 53, 56, 57, 61, 66, 147

beauty, 53, 56, 149

behavior, 1, 2, 4, 5, 6, 7, 10, 18, 19, 20, 26, 27, 39, 60, 64, 73, 76, 93

buddhism, 45

CAD, 6, 10, 20, 157

cellular automata, 27, 30, 31, 73, 151

chance, 49, 82

chicken and egg, 61

chinese, 17, 18, 23, 39, 40, 41, 43, 46, 56, 148, 149

chinese room, 17, 18, 23

chuang tzu, 48

code, 12, 26, 32, 66, 71, 78, 100, 151, 152, 153, 155, 156, 157

combinations, 13, 26, 34, 39, 43, 82, 90, 98, 154

complex, 2, 3, 5, 8, 9, 11, 13, 18, 19, 25, 27, 30, 33, 34, 39, 43, 73, 76, 155

complexity, 10, 17, 24, 25, 26, 27, 30, 33, 34, 35, 41, 59, 69, 82, 88, 93, 151, 155

computational, 26, 33, 35, 65

computationalism, 8, 9

computer graphics, 3, 7

conscious, 17, 19, 20, 21, 61, 148

consciousness, 9, 17, 18, 19, 20, 21, 23, 26, 33

contradiction, 21, 23, 24, 59

creativity, 9, 13, 30, 157

critical digital, 69, 151

dada, 26, 148

decision-making, 27

defeat, 52

definition, 5, 18, 19, 21, 22, 24, 25, 26, 30, 33, 34, 37, 39, 41, 42, 49, 53, 82, 93, 98, 147, 149, 150

design, 2, 3, 4, 5, 6, 7, 8, 9, 10, 11, 12, 13, 17, 20, 21, 22, 23, 24, 26, 30, 33, 34, 46, 47, 53, 54, 56, 60, 61, 62, 65, 66, 68, 69, 70, 71, 76, 78, 80, 82, 85, 86, 102, 108, 147, 149, 150, 152, 153, 154, 156, 157, 158

deterministic, 3, 27, 48

digital culture, 11, 59, 94

diphthongs, 42

discovery, 48

electronic, 2, 6, 10, 148

error, 3, 5, 45, 49

etymological, 39, 41, 46, 47

everything, 45, 47, 48, 49, 93, 94, 148

fallacy, 25

foreign, 8, 11, 19, 25, 34, 37, 48, 59

form, 3, 4, 6, 8, 19, 21, 22, 23, 26, 27, 32, 38, 40, 41, 48, 60, 64, 65, 69, 71, 94, 100, 148, 149, 150, 151, 155, 157

game, 8, 76

genius, 11, 17, 18, 20, 22, 23, 24, 26, 28, 30, 34, 54, 65, 152

Greek, 38, 39, 40, 41, 42, 43, 45, 46, 47, 56, 59, 92, 98, 149, 152, 153, 154, 155, 156, 158 haiku, 90

heuristic, 5, 6

humanistic, 11, 18, 146, 152, 155

hybrid, 12, 69

idea, 11, 17, 18, 20, 37, 45, 48, 51, 60, 64, 69, 93, 146, 151, 153, 157

ideal, 1

illusion, 20, 45, 47, 48, 56

impossible, 2, 8, 10, 18, 19, 21, 24, 34, 41, 48, 61, 80, 82, 156

index, 55

Indo-European, 55, 56, 57

intelligence, 5, 6, 8, 9, 13, 19, 20, 26, 33, 60, 80, 82, 93, 94, 156

irregular, 25

Kuhn, 37

language, 9, 26, 38, 41, 43, 47, 66, 69, 89, 90, 152, 153, 154, 155, 157

letter, 40, 41, 42, 43, 44, 147

life, 1, 42, 45, 48, 50, 55, 66, 146

Marcov, 26

match, 34, 82

mathematics, 1, 11, 27, 149

maya, 60, 61, 152, 153

mechanical, 6, 13, 19, 20, 80, 146

media, 2, 6, 10, 13, 35, 69, 149

medium, 3, 7, 8, 9, 19, 20, 154

memorization, 22, 65

memory, 2, 7, 9, 10, 47, 59, 153

meta, 23, 146, 153, 157

methodology, 149, 151

mind, 1, 2, 3, 4, 8, 17, 19, 20, 23, 24, 30, 35, 38, 76, 93, 146, 147, 148, 156

myths, 11, 17, 21, 23, 59, 155

name, 13, 32, 38, 52, 53, 149, 152

network topology, 108

new, 2, 3, 5, 6, 10, 11, 13, 22, 23, 26, 27, 32, 35, 38, 39, 40, 41, 42, 46, 47, 48, 50, 55, 57, 59, 65, 69, 81, 90, 93, 94, 146, 148, 149, 151, 154, 155, 157, 158

non-human, 8, 19, 81, 94, 155

nothing, 45, 46, 47, 48, 57, 61, 151, 153

nothingness, 45, 46

notion, 9, 11, 18, 21, 24, 34, 40, 45, 46, 47, 48, 54, 64, 65, 153

paradigm, 11, 13, 30, 37, 38, 47, 60, 80, 146

paradox, 17, 18, 19, 21, 23, 25, 56, 57, 59, 64

parametric, 149, 150, 151

parasight, 11, 37, 38, 39, 40

parasite, 37

Parmenides, 45, 46, 47, 56

Perault, 1

permutations, 11, 12, 13, 26, 82, 83, 85, 86, 88, 89, 90, 98, 99, 100, 101, 102, 105, 107, 108, 151, 154, 156

pixel, 7, 20

polynomial, 8, 19, 88

possible, 2, 3, 4, 5, 7, 8, 9, 10, 11, 12, 13, 18, 20, 21, 23, 26, 27, 33, 34, 37, 38, 39, 41, 42, 43, 45, 46, 47, 48, 49, 56, 57, 64, 69, 71, 80, 82, 83, 84, 85, 86, 87, 88, 89, 90, 98, 99, 100, 101, 102, 105, 108, 109, 110, 111, 148, 150, 151, 154

probabilistic, 3

problem-solving, 3, 8

program, 7, 10, 14, 19, 20, 22, 23, 65, 66, 69, 73, 82, 87, 88, 151, 153, 155, 156, 157, 158

programming, 66, 156, 157

puzzle, 81, 82, 151, 156

random, 2, 13, 21, 22, 25, 26, 27, 32, 33, 34, 49, 69, 71, 76, 80, 82, 85, 93, 147, 148, 149, 151

randomness, 1, 12, 21, 22, 23, 25, 26, 27, 30, 80, 147, 152

reality, 1, 3, 7, 10, 22, 45, 46, 47, 48, 56, 60, 61, 64, 65, 157

responsible, 17, 38, 49, 51

rules, 1, 2, 3, 5, 6, 7, 8, 9, 17, 19, 26, 27, 33, 41, 42, 76, 90, 154, 156 school, 45, 51, 62, 69, 70

Searle, 17, 18, 34

self-organization, 27

sentient, 26, 30

simulations, 2, 7, 10

socratic, 45, 46, 47, 48, 56

software, 11, 20, 23, 26, 33, 60, 65, 66, 69, 71, 78, 90, 146, 147, 148, 150, 151, 152, 153, 154, 155, 156

sport, 50

statue, 39, 52

stochastic, 27, 30, 32, 71, 73, 74, 78

story, 21, 23, 88, 90, 92, 93, 146, 147

superficial, 39, 78, 149, 150

symbol, 1, 17, 26, 34, 39, 40, 41, 44, 56, 89, 100

synthesize, 3, 7, 42

Taoism, 45

teach, 50, 157

theory, 3, 4, 5, 8, 56, 66, 78, 80, 81, 88, 151

Theseus, 59

truth, 2, 3, 8, 10, 19, 21, 23, 49

Turing, 18, 26, 93

unknown, 7, 10, 22, 24, 56, 156

unpredictable, 1, 3, 6, 7, 8, 13, 19, 25, 26, 34, 38, 60, 73, 80, 81, 147, 148, 154

value, 4, 11, 13, 17, 21, 23, 40, 41, 45, 48, 51, 65, 69, 110, 150, 155, 157

victory, 52

wedge, 44

word, 38, 39, 40, 41, 42, 44, 45, 46, 47, 56, 59, 61, 89, 98, 147, 148, 149, 152, 153, 156, 158

world, 1, 2, 3, 7, 9, 10, 11, 18, 22, 23, 24, 30, 34, 38, 40, 41, 45, 48, 60, 61, 65, 69, 71, 80, 81, 89, 90, 93, 94, 146, 148, 150, 151, 152, 153, 154, 156